INGVAR SØDER NIELSEN

Wooden Toys

Drawings and templates:
MARIANNE SCHULTZ

DAVID PORTEOUS
CHUDLEIGH DEVON

Acknowledgements
Many thanks to Transe Poulsen, Hammerum, who
made all the models shown in this book. Also
to Ragna Poulsen and Marianne Schultz who did
all the decoration work.

A CIP catalogue record for this book is
available from the British Library.

Published by David Porteous
PO Box 5
Chudleigh
Newton Abbot
Devon TQ13 0YZ

ISBN 0 870586 05 0

Translated by Tim Bowler

Printed in Hong Kong

CONTENTS

INTRODUCTION

Wood has always been used as a material for making tools, houses, furniture, vehicles, ships and all kinds of other articles that we use in our daily lives, so it is quite natural that we have come to use wood to make toys for children, and in many instances these toys are simply smaller versions of the things adults use.

Wood is an excellent material for toys. It is easy to work, very durable and, of course, beautiful to look at. But nowadays it can be costly to produce toys from wood, so other materials are often used. For example, a great many toys are now made from plastic, and they are certainly very realistic and accurate reproductions of some of the 'technical wonders' of our modern world. But plastic toys have a limited durability, and this inevitably causes great disappointment to young and old alike.

Wooden Toys offers tips and instructions on how to make simple, attractive and long-lasting wooden toys. It is my hope that the book will inspire you to start making your own wooden toys at home.

The book starts with a brief outline of the tools and materials you will need. Some people may think this section is unnecessary but I have included it in order to give children an idea of the most important working aids at their disposal. There are also instructions on how to decorate the models and how to enlarge the templates.

Against most of the headings you will see a number in brackets — for example [25]. This means that that particular model can be seen in a colour illustration on page 25.

Have fun!

Ingvar Søder Nielsen

TOOLS

This section includes brief descriptions of a number of different tools that are suitable for making wooden toys. Many homes will already possess most of these tools so you shouldn't need to incur too much expense before you can get started. For more specific, detailed descriptions of tools, you should consult some of the specialist books on the subject.

Drills

There are four different kinds of drill — breast drill, hand brace, electric drill and hand drill — that can be used according to the needs and nature of the work.

The breast drill, with its firm hand-grip and brace and the support-plate against the chest, permits safe and stable drilling. It also operates at two speeds. The twist bit can also be used, although this is normally for high-speed electric drills.

The hand brace can be used with many of the bits which have four-sided shanks — twist bits, centre bits, auger bits and tank cutters. Children can also manage the hand brace as long as they are shown clearly what to do, but it is important to remember that some types of bit are very sharp.

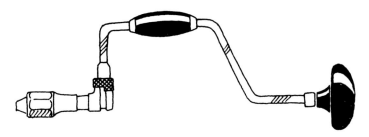

The electric drill obviously makes many jobs a great deal easier. For example, you can buy special screw bits for inserting screws. Never let children use an electric drill.

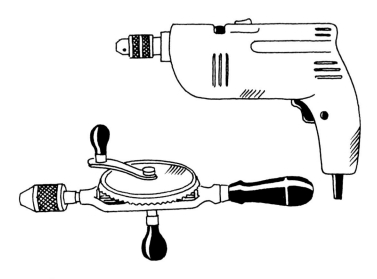

The hand drill is smaller and can only be used with bits up to 8 mm. It is rather difficult for children to handle.

Types of bit

The centre bit is used with the hand brace to make large holes, 10–40 mm in diameter. While you are drilling you have to press down on the hand-grip as the bit itself will not work its way through the wood. When the bit is half way in and the tip has broken through, turn the wood over and finish off by drilling from the other side.

The tank cutter can be used for making large or small wheels or, of course, holes of the same size. Two or three different sizes should cover most of the vehicle wheels you will want to make (see page 24).

The auger bit is fitted with a thread so that it works itself through the wood. Do not press down on the drill before the thread has broken through. Use this bit in the hand brace. You can also buy auger bits that can be adjusted so that you can drill holes of different diameters.

The twist bit is the most common type of bit. It is also called the metal bit. This is rather misleading because you can use it to drill all kinds of materials, including wood. The diameter of the bit is indicated on the round shank. You can also buy twist bits with four-sided shanks for use in the hand brace, but this type is not as precise as the twist bit with a round shank. When you are drilling with a twist bit, it is very important to clean off the chips, otherwise they 'pack in', and the bit can become too hot, burn the wood and lose its cutting capacity. Clean the bit by lifting it out of the hole while drilling. That way the chips will be thrown clear as the bit rotates, and you can continue with the drilling.

The countersink bit comes in many sizes and is used to countersink screws with flat heads (see page 14).

Tip: If you want to avoid ruining the reverse side of the wood while you are drilling, place another piece of wood underneath and fix the two pieces together.

centre bit

twist bit

tank cutter

auger bit

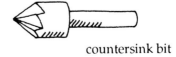

countersink bit

Wood file

You can use a wood file for lots of different jobs — rounding off corners, for example.

Tip: If the file is filled with chips, dip it in boiling water for a few moments. Then brush off the chips with a stiff brush. Dry the file thoroughly so that it does not rust.

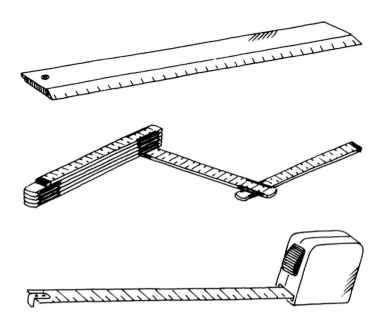

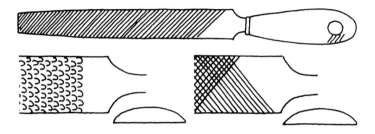

Hammer

A so-called Warrington hammer is handy for all kinds of jobs. You can use it either for small nails or for knocking wooden dowels and pieces of round wood. A small hammer is also useful for tapping in small tacks.

Bradawl

The bradawl is not a drill as such but is used for 'pricking' holes in the wood to give screws something to grip.

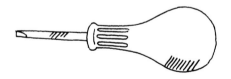

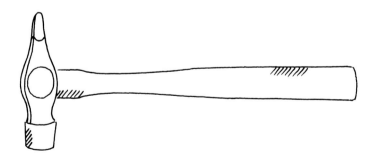

Saw

The coping saw is used in the same way as the fretsaw (see page 11) but it has a thicker and stronger blade and can therefore cut thicker wood than the fretsaw. If you are making your model from a piece of thick wood, it will be a long job if you use a coping saw, so it might be a good idea for an adult to cut out the model with a pad saw first, then the children can take over the rest of the job.

Tape measure

For measuring you can use a ruler, a folding rule or a tape measure.

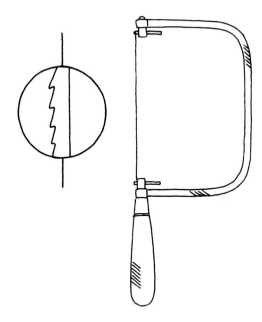

The fretsaw, with its thin blade and the large loop of the frame, is ideal for cutting out figures from thin pieces of wood. One advantage with the fretsaw is that you can sit down while you use it. It needs a certain amount of practice before you can become thoroughly confident with the fretsaw.

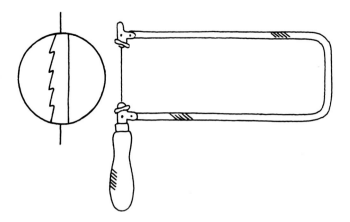

The hand saw is a strong saw with large teeth. It is particularly useful for sawing through sheets and boards.

Sawhorse

When you are working with the fretsaw or coping saw, you need to keep the wood steady in a sawhorse. The two models shown in the illustration can be set up in a carpenter's bench, in a vice, or on the edge of a table using a cramp (see page 12).

The back saw has a broad blade with small teeth and a strong, stiffened back. It is good for cutting smaller pieces of wood — for example in the mitre box (see page 12).

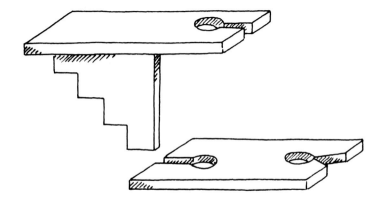

Screwdriver

The 'standard' screwdriver has a straight, flat blade and can be used for screws with a straight groove (see the illustration on page 14).

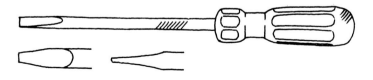

The Philips screwdriver has a blade that is in the shape of a star. It is extremely effective as it can grip the screw in four places (see the illustration on page 14).

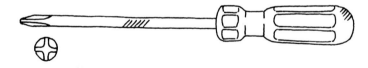

The Posidrive screwdriver is a special kind of screwdriver that grips the screw in eight places and allows you to screw it in extra tight.

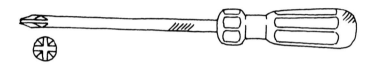

The Philips and Posidrive screwdrivers are commonly known as cross-head screwdrivers.

Mitre box

You can use the mitre box to cut off small boards and strips of wood, or saw the ends at angles — 45 degrees, for example. The back saw is very useful for this kind of work, but you can also use a hand saw.

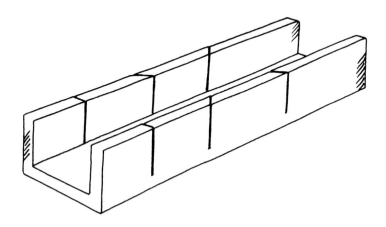

Cramp

This is used to hold fast two or more pieces of wood while you are working on them. You can also use it to hold two pieces of glued wood together until the glue is dry.

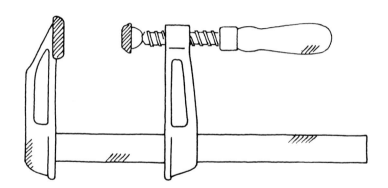

Stanley knife

A Stanley knife is an excellent tool for cutting, but it is dangerous for children to use on their own. If you are planning to use a Stanley knife, it is a good idea to make a cutting board (see the drawing).

When you are cutting, don't forget: Don't put your finger in front of the blade!

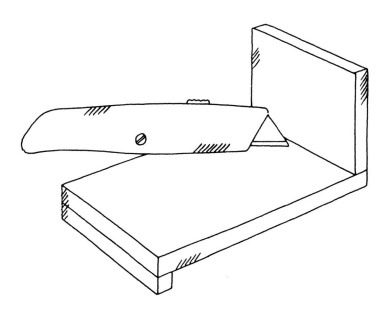

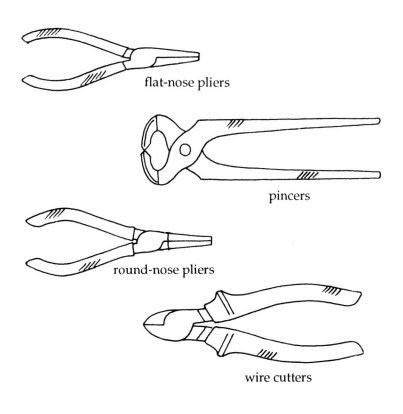

flat-nose pliers

pincers

round-nose pliers

wire cutters

Set squares

There are a number of different set squares. But a common set square with centimetres and 45 degrees marked on it will be sufficient.

Pliers

You can use the four different types of pliers — flat-nose pliers, pincers, round-nose pliers and wire cutters — for lots of useful things — pulling out nails, cutting wire, bending rods, making eye shapes and so on.

Tip: To avoid marking the wood when you are extracting nails, try placing a filling knife between the pincers and the wood.

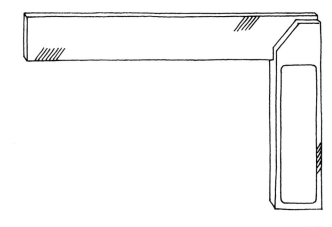

MATERIALS

Screws and nails

Slotted screws come in many sizes and have a variety of different heads and lengths of thread. Cross-head screws (see the illustration) also come in various sizes and have a number of different heads. They usually have a thread running all the way to the head. The flat-headed Philips screw, which is designed for countersinking, can also be seen in the illustration. There are also several different types of nail: round and square brads — tacks, clout nails, board nails, etc.

Tip: If you drive a brad 1–2 mm below the surface of the wood with a nail punch, you can 'close' the wood over the brad with a drop of water.

Using screws and nails

Before inserting the screw, it is a good idea to use a bradawl (see page 10). A flat-head screw should be countersunk 2–3 mm below the surface of the wood with the aid of a countersink bit (see page 9). Fill the hole with plastic wood. Nail ends can be flattened with a hammer to avoid splitting any fragile material. In the trade this is called 'closing' the nail. If there is less than 4 cm between each nail, be careful not to knock them into the same grain, otherwise you will run the risk of splitting the wood.

Tip: To stop screws or nails coming loose, it is sometimes a good idea to dip them in PVA-glue before knocking or screwing them in.

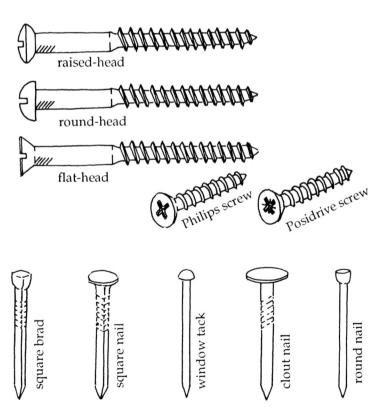

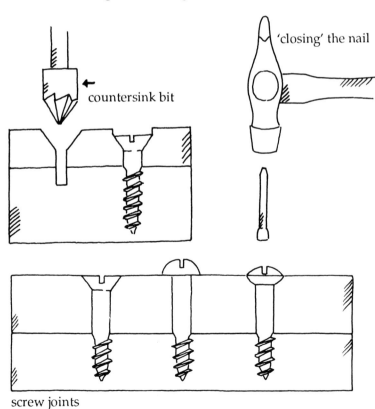

'closing' the nail

countersink bit

screw joints

Wood

Pine is used for many of the models in this book. It has many advantages: it is soft and it looks beautiful whether it is untreated, varnished or oiled. It will turn an attractive golden-brown colour with the passing of time. Pine can be glued using PVA-glue. Plywood (veneer) is also used in many places.

Although the models in this book are painted, many of the articles would look very attractive in high-grade untreated woods. Most of these are hardwoods and are therefore more difficult to work with than pine or plywood, but there is a wide range of beautiful kinds of wood that the more experienced woodworker can experiment with. There are, for example, several exciting native species that you can find either in gardens or in the countryside: birch, oak, elm, hazel, laburnum, white beech, chestnut, cherry, lime to name but a few. A wood such as laburnum is particularly worth mentioning because it is so strikingly beautiful. Within the space of a few centimetres it can range from delicate light-brown to black. It is not the kind of wood that you are likely to obtain from your local supplier, so you may have to find supplies for yourself.

There are also many very attractive exotic species: hickory, lemon tree, Cuban cedar, ebony, mahogany, Oregon pine, Brazilian rosewood, pitch pine, lignum vitae, teak, whitewood, etc. You can achieve some stunning effects by combining the different species. Remember that some of the species contain so much oil that it is impossible to glue them with ordinary PVA-glue. Ask your specialist supplier which types of glue should be used with the various species.

What size?

You can buy wood in several different thicknesses. If we talk of 18 mm pine, this means that the wood is 18 mm thick. Most of the models in this book use pine or plywood. Pine comes in the following thicknesses: 18 mm, 25 mm, 32 mm, 38 mm, 50 mm and 63 mm. Plywood comes in: 4 mm, 6 mm, 9 mm, 12 mm, 16 mm, 18 mm and 22 mm. Pieces of round wood, dowels, which are used, among other things, for wheels, come in the following diameters: 9 mm, 12 mm, 16 mm, 18 mm, 22 mm, 25 mm and 28 mm. There are thicker pieces of round wood but shops do not always have them in stock.

For the yo-yo on page 79 a piece of round wood with a diameter of 53 mm is used. The locomotives on pages 32 and 34 use a piece of round wood with a diameter of 43 mm. Don't forget that wood is a living material which contracts when it becomes dry. For that reason it is a good idea to measure pieces of round wood before using them so as to be quite sure of the dimensions. If you need thinner pieces of dowel than the above, it may be easier to go to a florist and buy some of the sticks used for binding flowers.

TECHNIQUES

Gluing the wood

Smooth and sanded wood surfaces can be glued together by applying PVA-glue (wood glue), which is very strong, to both sides. You can buy the glue at a DIY store or builder's merchant. Press the surfaces firmly together in a carpenter's bench or with cramps. The glue dries after 20 minutes but takes 6 hours to harden. PVA-glue is water-soluble, so you must not use it for models that are going to stand outside. For that you need special glue. Brushes that have been used to apply glue can be cleaned in water. If you keep your glue brushes in water, remember to squeeze all the water from them thoroughly before using them again, otherwise you will be in danger of thinning the glue. Some of the high-grade species of wood contain so much oil that you cannot use PVA-glue with them (see page 15).

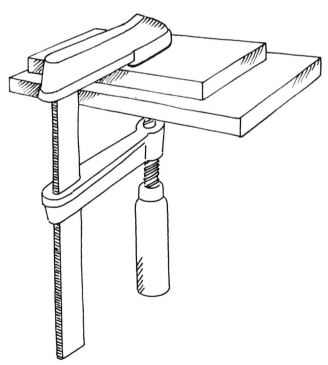

Cutting holes

If you want to cut out a large piece — a window in a car or a house, for example — first drill a hole inside the area marked for the window (see illustration). For sawing use a fretsaw or a coping saw (see pages 10 and 11). Undo the saw blade, run it through the hole and make it fast again. Then saw carefully along the line, at the same time revolving the wood so that the blade does not twist.

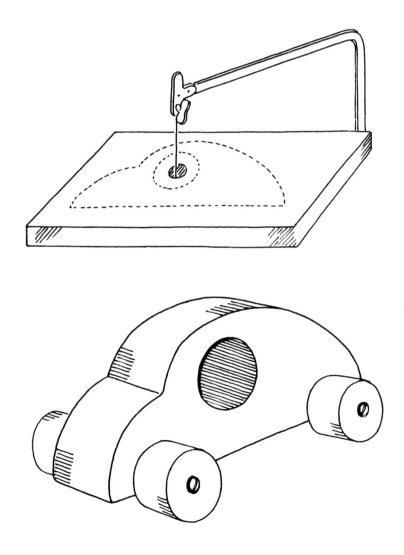

DECORATION

As you can see from the illustrations, decorating the toys is an important part of this book. There are many different kinds of paint and colouring that you can use for decoration. Unfortunately space does not allow us to go into all the different varieties in this book. However, you can usually get plenty of tips and good advice from your local craft shop and builder's merchant. If you want to achieve a really professional result, you must be very careful, especially in the basic treatment of the wood (see below). But, of course, you can also go 'over the top', so it is really up to you to decide how far you want to go with the work. All of the models in this book were painted with acrylic paint. The small, fine lines and decorations were drawn with 'paint pens' (see following page). All the models are treated with a primer and finally coated with clear, water-based varnish.

Basic and surface treatment

The surface of the wood should be cleaned and sanded with sandpaper before being painted or varnished. Basically sandpaper falls into three categories: coarse, medium and fine. Hold the sandpaper round a polishing block. Make sure you don't use sandpaper that is too coarse because it can cause deep scratches in the wood. Always remember to polish along the grain in the wood to avoid marking the wood. Even fine scratches will be visible when the wood is painted.

Next you can apply primer to the wood if you don't want to varnish or stain. When the wood is painted the grain swells so you have to polish it again with fine sandpaper. Holes in the surface — such as knots — can be stopped with filler or plastic wood. Before applying the decorative paint, the filler should be smoothed to an even finish. A complete, profes-

sional finish comes from smoothing, priming, smoothing again, filling, smoothing, painting, smoothing yet again and then painting. You may need to apply a third coat of paint if the article is not completely covered.

If you follow the method outlined above, you can be sure of a soft, velvety, uniform surface. To save on the painting and to give the model more 'life', you can finish off with a coat of clear water-based varnish.

Don't forget, of course, that toys are made to be played with and they are going to be exposed to knocks and scratches. So you don't always need to 'go to town' on the decoration.

Painting

The surface of the wood will determine which type of paint you will use. Rough, untreated surfaces can be easily covered with a wood stain or with poster colours. These work well on untreated wood, but it is sensible to polish the wood before you paint it. (see previous page). Planed or polished wood surfaces can be treated with matt, semi-matt or gloss acrylic paint. It is not a good idea to used oil-based paint. First, it is poisonous and second, it is difficult to work with. Non-toxic, 'child-safe' paints are now available, although in only limited colours.

If you're handy with your fingers you can mix your own colours from the red, yellow, green and blue paints. These can be toned with black and white. Make sure that they are pure, unmixed primary colours, and remember that the colours often turn a different shade as they dry. The safest way is to buy ready-mixed colours at a craft shop or a paint dealer. Many stores now offer special hobby sets with a range of colours in small quantities. It is very practical, when painting the models, to keep the paint in small foil trays. That way the paint pots can be kept closed so that no skin or remains of paint forms on the edges.

When the surface has been painted, you can draw the contours and smaller sections with 'paint pens'. These are available from some craft shops and art suppliers and they come in all colours. They contain a special kind of paint, which is released as you press the tip of the pen. They are much easier to use than a brush and give the contours a much sharper definition. All of the thin lines and patterns in this book have been drawn with these special pens. They help to give the models a smart, finished appearance. When you work with these pens you will soon discover how easy it is to give the models a thoroughly decorative appearance. However, they are not suitable for painting larger surfaces, because they run out too quickly.

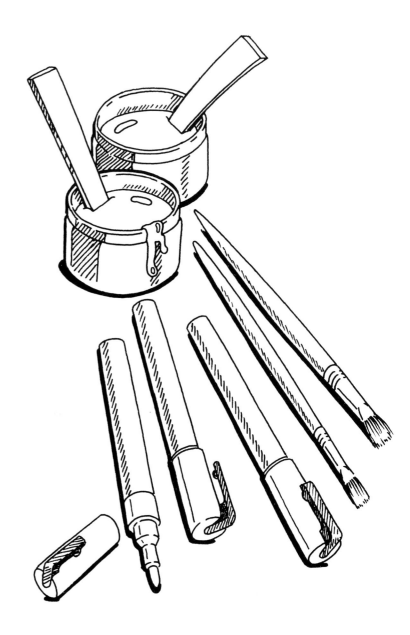

TEMPLATES

Most of the models in this book are based on templates, which are then transferred to the wood. Only in a few instances are the templates drawn full size. You will, therefore, need to enlarge the drawings until you reach the right size. The templates are drawn on a square grid, and each set of instructions will explain what the square represents. All the squares in the book are 1x1 cm. If, for example, the instructions say that the templates are drawn to a scale of 1:4, it means that a grid should be drawn with the same number of squares as the template, but that now each square should be 4x4 cm (see the illustration).

You begin by choosing where on the template drawing you are going to start, then find the corresponding pattern on the square grid. The points where the lines of the grid cross the pattern should be marked and the two points joined with a line as on the template drawing. Now the template can be plotted step by step.

If you want to use a template from the book in the original size, you can draw it on tracing paper. Transfer the template drawings to the wood with the help of carbon paper. If you have access to a photocopier with a facility for enlarging, you obviously will not need to use the square grid method.

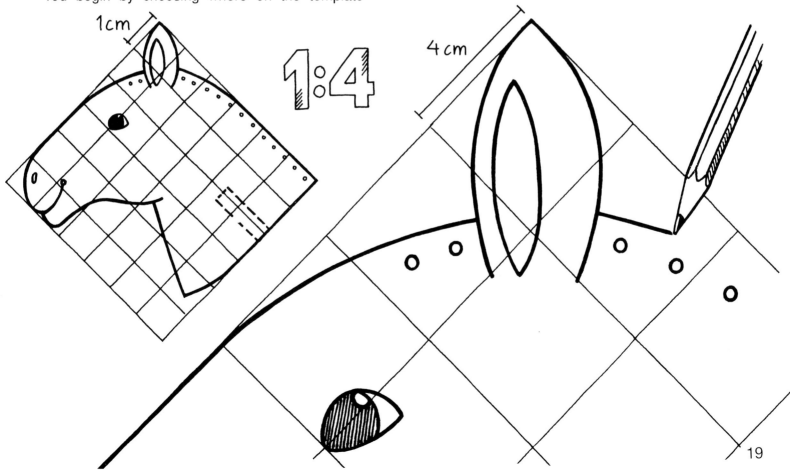

BUILDINGS

There are several different ways of making buildings out of wood. In this section we will see how to make three basic models, which can be varied or combined. For example, you could make a church or a farm (see pages 22 and 23).

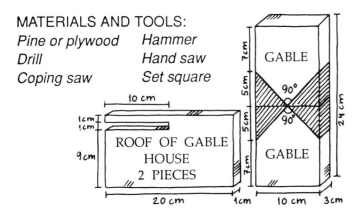

MATERIALS AND TOOLS:

Pine or plywood Hammer
Drill Hand saw
Coping saw Set square

Gable house [45]

The gable house is uncomplicated and easy to make. You can take it apart and reassemble it without having to use nails or screws. The house consists of two gables and two roof surfaces. The wood used for the gables should ideally be 2–3 cm thick — for example, you could use 25 mm pine. If the wood is thinner, the house will be less stable.

Mark the gables on the wood. If you follow the measurements on the drawings, which are suitable for making a little town house, you will need a piece of wood 10x24 cm. Shade the waste parts of the wood that are to be sawn off. The gables can vary in size, but they should always form an angle of 90 degrees in order to match the construction of the roof. Make the roof from two pieces of wood — 9 mm plywood, for example. Cut the grooves with a hand saw or coping saw and put the two half-sections of the roof together.

House with sides [45]

Unlike the gable house this house has sides. Saw out the gables as described in the previous section, but here they do not need to be more than 1 cm thick. Saw the roof and sides from 6 mm plywood. If you want to make the roof in the same way as the gable house, the grooves should not be more than 6 mm wide. Alternatively you can nail together the roof as shown in the illustration. In the instructions for the farm on page 22 and the church on page 23 the roof sections are nailed together. To make the roof slope equally on both sides, one roof section should be 6 mm wider than the other. If necessary you can strengthen the roof on the inside with a short four-sided strip of wood, 1x1 cm. You can either place the roof unfastened on top of the house or nail it down. If you are making a farm, it is a good idea not to fasten the roof because it is then easy to put in and take out the animals. The sides of the house should be about 5 mm shorter than the vertical section of the gable so that the roof will fit properly. Nail the sides to the gables.

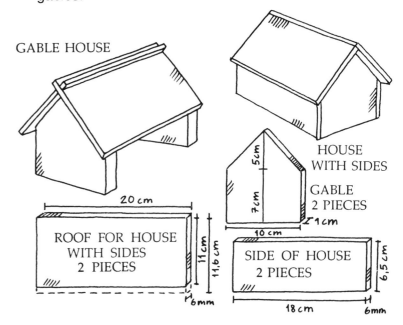

Houses made from blocks [25]

The simplest houses are made from 'blocks'. Narrow houses can be cut from 32 mm pine and wide houses from 63 mm pine. Cut the upper section of the block so that it is pointed to resemble a roof. If necessary you can cut roof surfaces from 4 mm plywood and nail them on (see illustration). The roofs should protrude slightly over the sides. The narrow high-rise blocks have no roofs (see illustration opposite). You can also make a tower from a 53 mm thick piece of round wood.

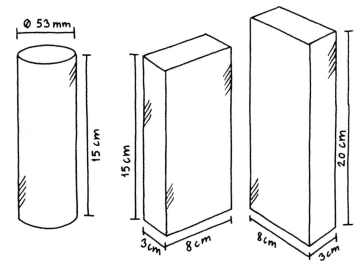

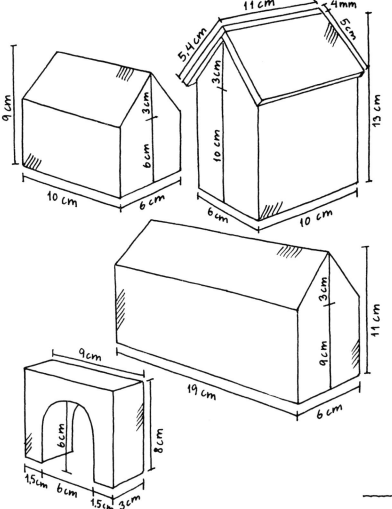

Decoration

You can decorate each individual house in an entirely different way. There is a wide range of possibilities: shops with signs — for example, FLORIST, FISH SHOP, BUTCHER or SUPERMARKET; high-rise blocks with plenty of windows and different coloured curtains; town houses with smart front doors and large windows; and farm cottages with flowers in the windows and red-tiled roofs.

Farm [45]

To make a set of farm buildings consisting of two stables and a main house, you will need: six gables for the stable buildings and main house; four sides for the stable buildings; two narrow and two wide roof sections for the stable buildings; two sides for the main house; one narrow and one wide roof section for the main house. All the measurements are shown in the drawings, and the buildings are assembled as described on page 20. On page 43 you will find instructions on how to make animals for the farm.

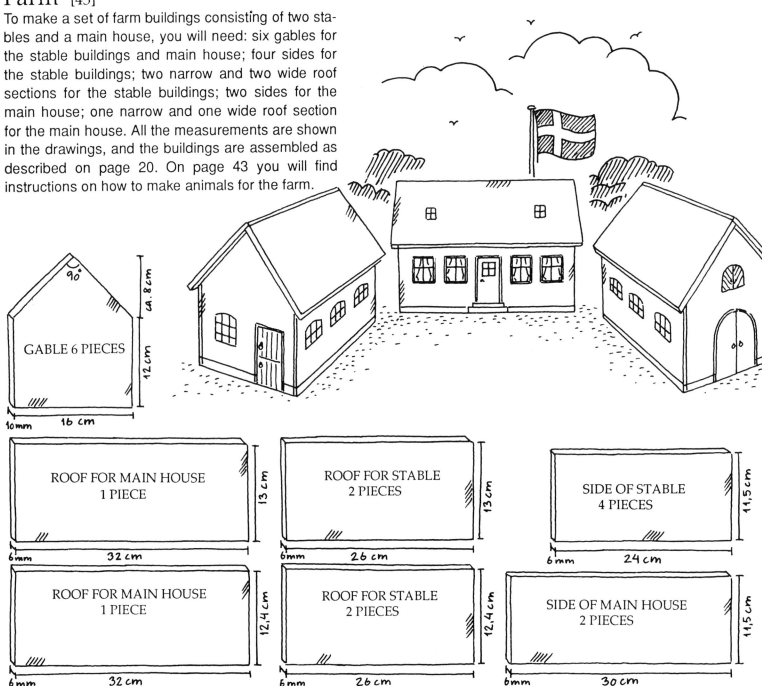

GABLE 6 PIECES
90°
ca. 8 cm
12 cm
10 mm
16 cm

ROOF FOR MAIN HOUSE
1 PIECE
13 cm
6 mm
32 cm

ROOF FOR STABLE
2 PIECES
13 cm
6 mm
26 cm

SIDE OF STABLE
4 PIECES
11,5 cm
6 mm
24 cm

ROOF FOR MAIN HOUSE
1 PIECE
12,4 cm
6 mm
32 cm

ROOF FOR STABLE
2 PIECES
12,4 cm
6 mm
26 cm

SIDE OF MAIN HOUSE
2 PIECES
11,5 cm
6 mm
30 cm

Church [45]

The church consists of a steeple and a nave. To make it you will need: two gables for the steeple; two sides for the steeple; one wide and one narrow roof section for the steeple; two gables for the nave; two sides for the nave; one wide and one narrow roof section for the nave. Assemble the church as described on page 20. So that you can push the nave right up against the steeple, the roof protrudes over the gable at one end only (see illustration).

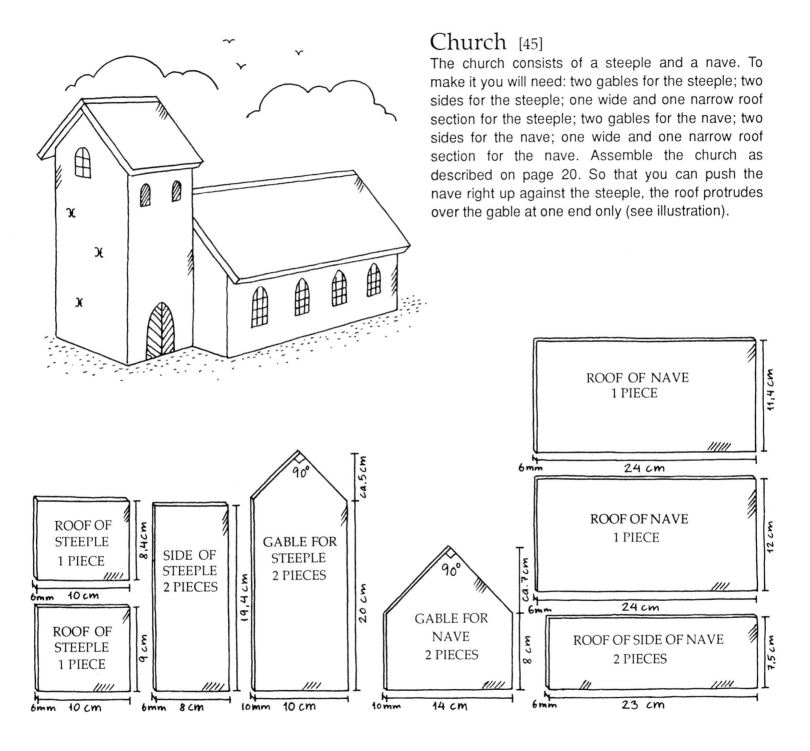

ROOF OF NAVE
1 PIECE
11,4 cm
6mm 24 cm

ROOF OF NAVE
1 PIECE
12 cm
6mm 24 cm

ROOF OF STEEPLE
1 PIECE
8,4 cm
6mm 10 cm

SIDE OF STEEPLE
2 PIECES
19,4 cm
6mm 8 cm

GABLE FOR STEEPLE
2 PIECES
90°
ca. 5 cm
20 cm
10mm 10 cm

GABLE FOR NAVE
2 PIECES
90°
ca. 7 cm
8 cm
10mm 14 cm

ROOF OF STEEPLE
1 PIECE
9 cm
6mm 10 cm

ROOF OF SIDE OF NAVE
2 PIECES
7,5 cm
6mm 23 cm

MOTOR VEHICLES

All the vehicles are made from the same basic model. This makes it easier to rationalize 'production' as the real motor vehicle manufacturers do. This section starts by explaining the simplest way to make wheels for the various models you will find in the book.

MATERIALS AND TOOLS:
Pine
Ornamental nails for lights
Dowel, 9 and 18 mm
Washers (to place between the wheels)
Wooden wheels (see below)
Drill
Coping saw
Hand saw
Mitre box

Making the wheels

With the help of a tank cutter you can cut a wheel out of a piece of wood. Start by marking the outline of the wheel, then position the tip of the drill in the centre and drill half way through. Turn over the wood and finish the drilling from the other side. Sandpaper or file away any splinters.

You can also make wheels from pieces of dowel of varying thicknesses (see page 15). The measurements stated on the models do not always match the standard thicknesses of round wood. Obviously you should use the piece that is nearest to the measurements given. Most of the wheels are about 1 cm thick. First drill holes for the wheel axle, then saw the dowel into suitably sized discs in the mitre box.

You can make wheels that will turn but it takes a little practice to do this (see page 26). You can also strengthen the wheels with wheel bearings made from brass lining pieces. Enlarge each lining piece with a nail punch hammer. This will tighten it in the hole (see illustration below). For wheel axles you can use thin dowel. Alternatively, try using screws.

When you fit the wheels, it is a good idea to insert a washer between them and the car to make them run more freely. During assembly it is best to drill the body with a twist bit 1 mm less than the diameter of the screw (measured under the head of the screw). Push the screw through the wheel before dipping it in glue and screw it into the hole you have drilled. When the glue is dry it will stop the screw from rotating. Of course, you can use circular articles — coins, buttons and washers — as wheels.

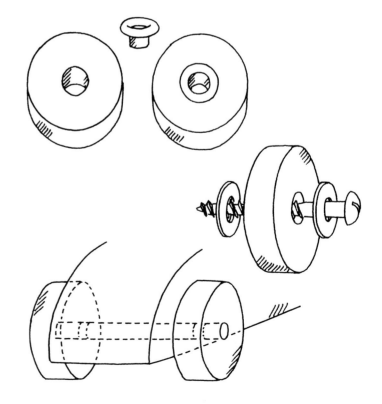

Houses made from blocks, page 21. Bus, page 26.
Lorry, page 27. Family car and racing car, page 31.

Turning the wheels

It is a little more complicated to make wheels that turn — and it's not something children should try. First, make the blocks of wood as round as possible. Screw the discs together on a long screw and saw its head off with a hacksaw. Hold the long screw securely in a drill (see illustration). It is sensible to fasten the discs together with a blob of glue so that they do not slip during rotation. When you start drilling, make sure you get a good grip. Now you can round off the wheels with a wood file or a sanding cork with coarse sandpaper. The wheels that have been glued together can be sawn apart in the mitre box. Finish off by smoothing the surface with fine sandpaper.

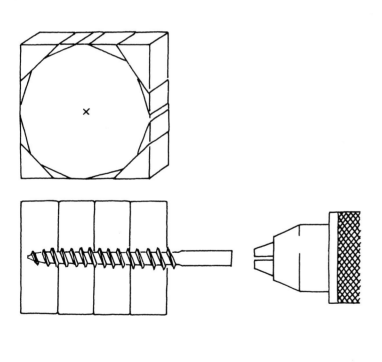

Bus [25] [29]

For the bus you need a block of wood 20x8x6 cm. Fit six wheels, 2.5 cm in diameter, directly onto the block. Round off the edges of the bus with sandpaper or a wood file.

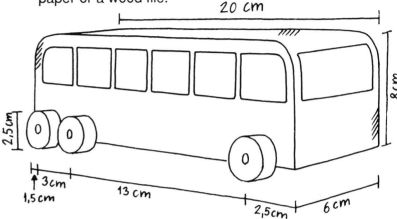

London bus [29]

Make the characteristic double-decker bus from a block of wood 20x14x6 cm. Fit six wheels, 2.5 cm in diameter, directly onto the block. Round off the edges of the bus with sandpaper or a wood file.

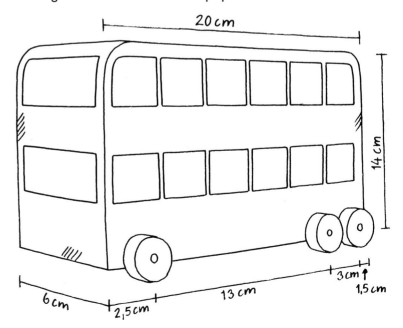

Lorry [25] [29]

The lorry consists of a driver's cab and a body. The body should be 20x6x2 cm. The driver's cab is a block of wood 5x6x6 cm, which is sawn at an angle as you can see from the illustration. Use two blocks to hold the wheels. The front block should be 6x3x1 cm, and the rear block 6x8x1 cm. The body of the lorry should be made from strips of wood. The measurements are shown on the illustration. Assemble the vehicle and nail the strips of wood in position as shown. The wheels of the lorry should be 4 cm in diameter and should be fitted as shown in the illustration. Using the lorry as a basic model, you can also make a vehicle with a ladder so that it can help with firefighting.

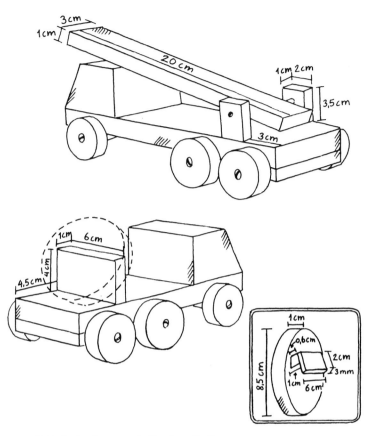

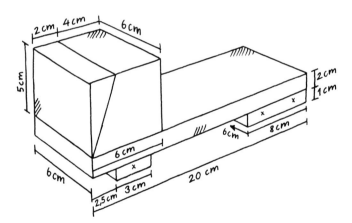

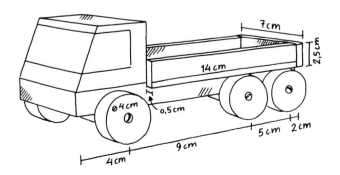

Vehicle with ladder [29]

The basic model is a lorry without its body; see opposite for the dimensions. The two blocks of wood used to hold the ladder should be 3.5x2x1 cm. Nail the blocks in position as shown. The ladder should be 20x3x1 cm. It is extremely difficult to saw out the rungs of the ladder so a better plan is to paint them in when you come to decorate the vehicle. To fit the ladder, drill holes in the two blocks about 1 cm from the upper edge. Then drill holes through the ladder about 2 cm from the end. Use a piece of thin dowel or two screws as an axle so that you can move the ladder to an upright position.

You can also make a radar vehicle with a radar screen on the body (see illustration).

Truck [29]

Make the base section, the chassis, from a piece of wood 16x6x2 cm. The driver's cab is the same size as that of the lorry (see page 27). Mark the correct position on the base section. Just behind the driver's cab drill two holes, 1 cm deep, in the base section. Glue two pieces of 10 mm dowel, 8 cm long into the holes to act as exhaust pipes. Then glue and nail the driver's cab to the base section.

The six wheels of the truck are 4 cm in diameter and are mounted on blocks as outlined in the section on lorries (see page 27).

Drill a hole for the trailer in the body of the truck. This hole should be about 11 mm in diameter and 1.5 cm deep.

Make the trailer from a block 20x6x6 cm. Mount the wheel block, 9x6x3 cm, at the back under the trailer. The trailer has 4 wheels, 4 cm in diameter, fitted as in the illustration. It couples by means of a 10 mm diameter dowel, 2.5 cm long, mounted in the trailer as shown.

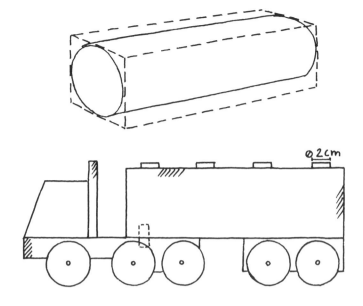

Tanker [45]

You can convert the truck to a tanker by rounding off the trailer to resemble a tank. Saw off the corners as in the illustration above and smooth the edges with a wood file or sandpaper until the tank is completely round.

Alternatively, you can use a thick, round piece of wood. Saw the caps from a 2 cm piece of dowel and glue them to the top of the tank.

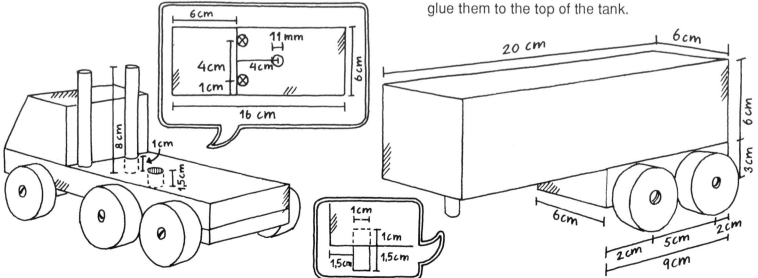

Truck, page 28. Vehicle with ladder and Radar vehicle, page 27. Jeep, page 30.

Lorry, page 27. Loader tractor, page 30.

Houses made from blocks, page 21. Buses, page 26. Car and caravan and Racing car, page 31.

Jeep [29]

You need three sections to make a jeep. The base section is 12x6x2 cm. The bonnet is 6x6x1 cm. The rear section is 6x3x1.5 cm. Glue and nail the bonnet and rear section to the base section as shown. To fit the wheels use two blocks, 6x1x1 cm, and glue and nail them under the base section.

The jeep has five wheels, 3 cm in diameter. One is a spare, and this is screwed on at the back. The other four wheels are fitted on the blocks. For the steering wheel use a smaller wheel, 2 cm in diameter. Screw or glue it on as shown.

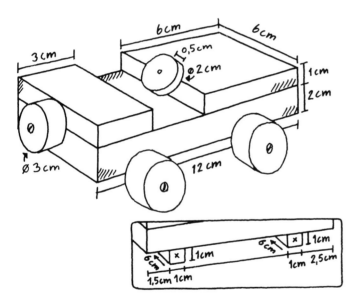

Tractor [45]

For the tractor you need two blocks, one 4x6x6 cm and the other 12x6x5 cm. Both blocks are cut at an angle as you can see from the illustration. Glue and nail the smaller block onto the bigger one to act as the driver's cab. For the exhaust pipe use a 9 mm piece of dowel, 3.5 cm long. Fit the dowel as shown in the illustration. Attach the two small wheels, 3 cm in diameter, to a block 6x2x2 cm, then glue and nail this in position. Screw the two big wheels, 8 cm in diameter, directly onto the larger block as shown.

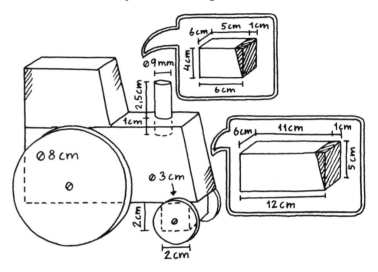

Loader tractor [29]

The loader tractor is a tractor with a shovel. Make the shovel from two pieces of wood, 6x5x1 cm and 6x4x1 cm, glued and nailed together. The arms are made from two strips of wood, 11x1x1 cm. Fit these on the loader tractor using screws and, if necessary, washers to help them move freely. Then glue and nail the arms to the shovel as shown in the illustration.

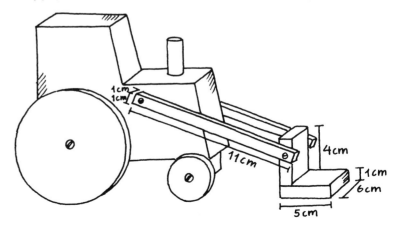

Car and caravan [29]

The little round car and the caravan are made from two pieces of wood, 12.5x5.5x6 cm. The window holes should be 3 cm in diameter. It is easier to control the wood if you drill these holes before shaping the model. The wheels, which are 2.5 cm in diameter, are mounted directly onto the models. The edges of the models can be rounded off with a wood file or sandpaper.

You can, if you prefer, paint on the windows as it is difficult to drill a hole through such a thick piece of wood. Join the caravan to the car with a hook and eye.

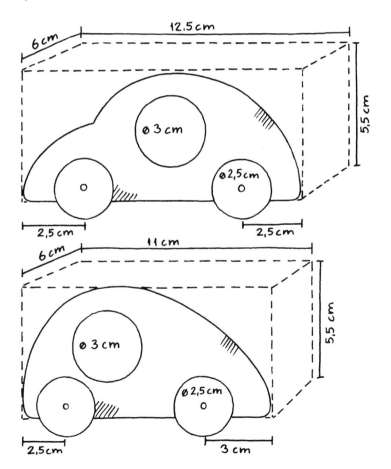

Racing car [25] [29]

Make the racing car from a piece of wood 15x5.5x6 cm. Drill the window hole, 3 cm in diameter, before cutting out the model so that you have more control over the wood. Instead of drilling the hole you can paint the window on as part of the decoration. When you have cut out the racing car, fit the four wheels, 2.5 cm in diameter, directly onto the model. You can round off the edges of the car with a wood file or sandpaper.

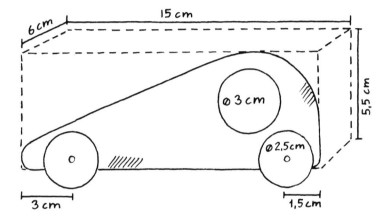

Decoration

For bumpers you can use small, 5 mm strips of wood. Glue and nail the bumpers front and back. For lights you could try using small tacks with large round heads or ornamental brass nails, but these are optional extras. When you paint the vehicles, don't forget that contractors' machines are usually yellow. They also have the company name smartly displayed on the side. Paint the window sections in contrasting colours, and, if you have time, try painting details such as mudguards, small number plates, wheels with rims and so on.

TRAINS

The old steam trains with smoke billowing from their chimneys have always been a source of fascination. They looked so impressive as they came chugging through the countryside, leaving a plume of black and grey smoke behind them. And when the chief engineer peeped the whistle at full power the sound was deafening. It's old locomotives like these that are the starting-point for the models in this section.

MATERIALS AND TOOLS:

Hooks and eyes
Ornamental nails for lights
Dowel, 9 and 43 mm
Washers (to place between the wheels)
Drill
Hammer
Hand saw

Steam train [33]

The locomotive is built together with the coal tender on a base section 24x4x2 cm. The piece of dowel used for the locomotive is 43 mm in diameter and 13 cm long. The driver's section is a block 4x4x6 cm, and the roof is 6x6x1 cm. The coal tender is a block 4x4x6 cm. The two cylinders at the front of the train are 9 mm pieces of dowel, 2 cm long. Each cylinder can be fitted with a flat-head nail to represent the 'buffer'. The chimneys are 9 mm pieces of dowel and are drilled 1.5 cm down in the boiler. The front chimney is 4 cm long, and the two behind it are 2.5 cm long. Fit the chimneys as shown in the illustration. The 16 wheels are 2 cm and 3 cm in diameter. Attach the wheels as shown in the illustration.

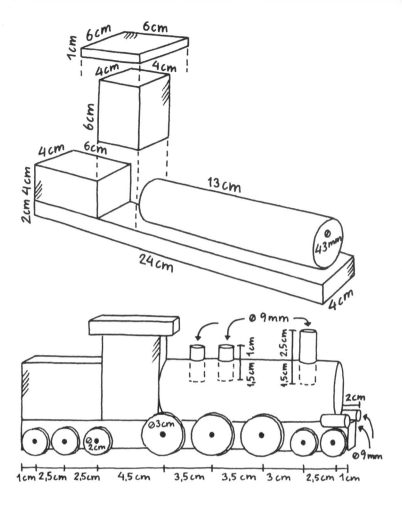

Coal wagon or tender [33]

For the base of the tender saw a piece of wood 6.5x4x2 cm. At the top glue and nail a block 6.5x4x4 cm. Fit the four wheels, which are 3 cm in diameter, as shown in the illustration.

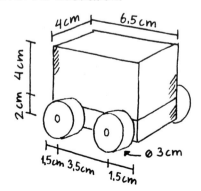

Houses made from blocks, page 21. Trains, pages 32–34.

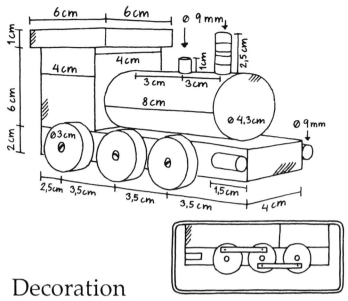

Shunting engine [33]

The shunting engine is built on a base section, 13x4x2 cm. The driver's cab is a block 4x4x6 cm and the roof is 6x6x1 cm. Make the boiler from a 43 mm piece of dowel, 8 cm long. Fit the two cylinders at the front of the train as described in the section on steam trains on page 32. Saw the chimneys from a 9 mm piece of dowel, 2.5 and 4 cm long, and assemble them as shown in the diagram. Fit the six wheels, 3 cm in diameter, also as shown. If you want to add rods to the wheels, you can glue on thin pieces of dowel, but these will prevent the wheels from turning.

Carriages [33]

You can make passenger coaches with separate compartments from blocks, 24x8x4 cm. The roof is 25x5x1 cm. Each carriage needs eight wheels, 2 cm in diameter, fitted as shown in the illustration.

If you want to make a low-loader, use a base section 24x4x2 cm. Fit the wheels as described above.

Decoration

Paint the trains black but give the chimneys red and white stripes. Paint the carriages and rolling stock in whatever colours you wish. You can paint stripes and windows on the carriages or write on the side if you wish. If you prefer to maintain the older style in keeping with the locomotives, paint the carriages in the livery of one of the pre-nationalization companies. You can make the lights for the train from ornamental nails or pieces of 9 mm round wood cut into thin discs. Use hooks and eyes to couple the different carriages together.

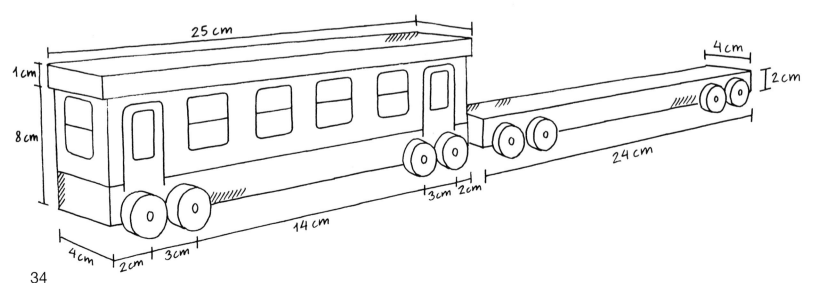

SHIPS

There are many types of ship which you can make from wood, including the characteristic passenger ferries together with fishing boats, coasters and container ships.

MATERIALS AND TOOLS:
Pine
Dowel, 3 and 9 mm
Drill
Hammer
Hand saw

You can use the base section on page 36 for the container ship, oil tanker and cargo vessel. The base is about 1 cm thick and can be cut from a piece of pine 20x5 cm. If you want to make the ship shorter or longer, you can modify the length of the base section. You may wish to make the vessel taper towards the stern; if so, you can saw the corners backwards at an angle, but be careful not to alter any of the dimensions of the different blocks.

Container ship [37]

Cut out the base section as described above. You will also need four blocks, A–D, and a mast. A is 5x4x1 cm. B is 3x2.5x1 cm. C is 5x3x1.5 cm. D is 7x1.5x1.5 cm. Glue and nail together the blocks as shown. Make the two masts from thin dowel. One piece should be 7 cm long, and the other 4.5 cm. Fit the masts to the vessel by drilling through the block.

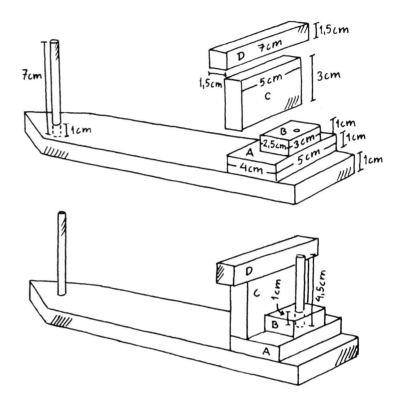

Oil tanker [37]

You build the oil tanker in the same way as the container ship, but this vessel has two extra blocks, E and F. E is 5x2x2 cm. F is 10x1x1 cm. Assemble the blocks as shown.

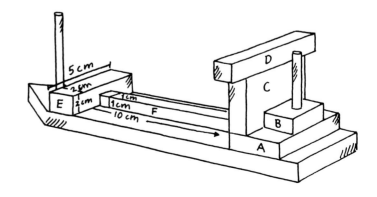

Cargo boat [37]

Cut out the base section as shown in the layout below. You should also use six blocks, A–F, and a chimney G. A is 5x4x1.5 cm. B is 1.5x3x3.5 cm. C is 5x3x1.5 cm. D is 4.5x2x1.5 cm. E is 7x2x1.5 cm. F is 5x2x1.5 cm. G is a 9 mm piece of dowel, 2cm long. Assemble the different parts as shown. The two masts are thin pieces of dowel, 7 cm and 4.5 cm long, and they should be fitted as outlined in the section on container ships on page 35.

Fishing boat [37]

The base section of the fishing boat is shown below. The base is approximately 1 cm thick and can be cut from pine, 17x5 cm. This boat is easy to make as it consists only of a base, a wheel house, a cabin and a mast. The wheel house is 5x4.5x3.5 cm. The cabin is 2x2x2 cm. Cut the block at an angle as shown in the illustration. For the mast use thin dowel, 8 cm long. Assemble the parts as shown.

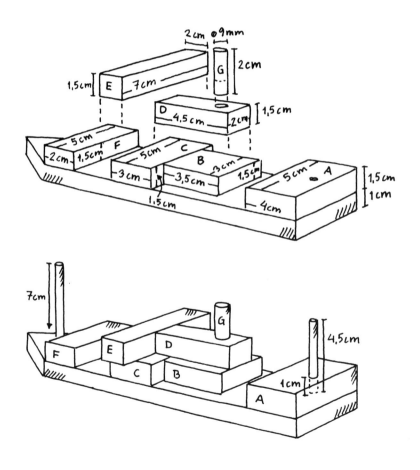

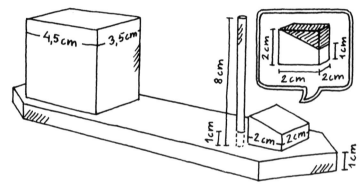

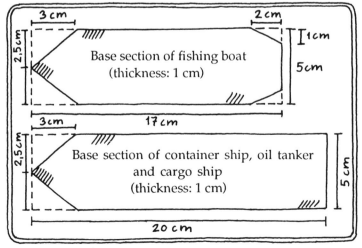

Houses made from blocks, page 21. Ships, page 35–38.

Passenger ferry [37]

Cut the base section from 18 mm pine (see the template). This section should be 35x12 cm. The two sides are 19x6x1 cm. The top section is 19x12x1 cm. The two blocks are 12x4x2 cm. The funnel is 5x4x2 cm. The smoke pipe on top of the funnel is sawn from 19 mm dowel, 1 cm long. The two masts, which are 8 cm long, are sawn from 10 mm dowel. Assemble the different parts as shown in the illustration.

Decoration

It looks very stylish if you can paint in small details on the ships. You could paint the ferry black and white, and fishing boats are often white and blue. If you want to go a little further, you could make small lifeboats for the ferry and attach flags to the masts.

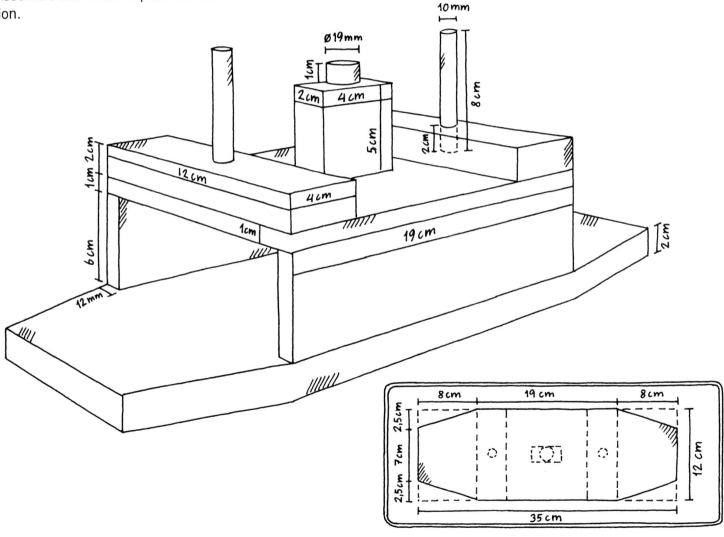

AIRCRAFT

Away from the towns you can find airports which are busy with both civilian and military aircraft. Here there are routine passenger aircraft taking people from one place to another, and there are also fighters, helicopters, vintage planes, monoplanes, biplanes and triplanes.

MATERIALS AND TOOLS:
Plywood, 4 mm
Pine, 18 mm
Ice lolly stick for the propeller (or 4 mm plywood)
Dowel, 10 and 16 mm
Welding wire, 3 mm
Drill
Coping saw
Hand saw
Back saw
Mitre box
Wire cutters
Set square

The basic template for the fuselage of the aircraft on page 40 is drawn half-size. Cut out the fuselage in 18 mm pine. You can round off the edges with sandpaper, but make sure that the vintage planes have a more angular fuselage than the modern ones. Cut out the various wings in 4 mm plywood in accordance with the templates on page 40, then glue and nail them to the fuselage of the plane. You will find all the other templates on the same page.

If you wish, you can fit wheels to the aircraft by nailing a 2x1x1 cm block under the fuselage. Screw the wheels, which should be about 2 cm in diameter, to the block.

Fighter [41]

The fighter is fitted with 'delta wings', see page 40, and two jet engines which are made from 10 mm dowel. You can see where to position the wings and jet engines from the illustration.

Passenger plane [41]

The passenger plane is fitted with jet engines, which are made from four pieces of 10 mm dowel. Glue and nail the jet engines under the wings (see illustration).

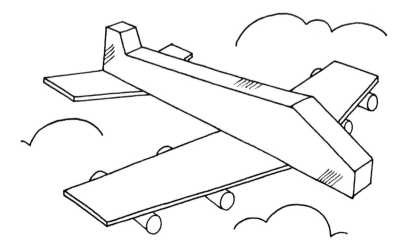

1:2

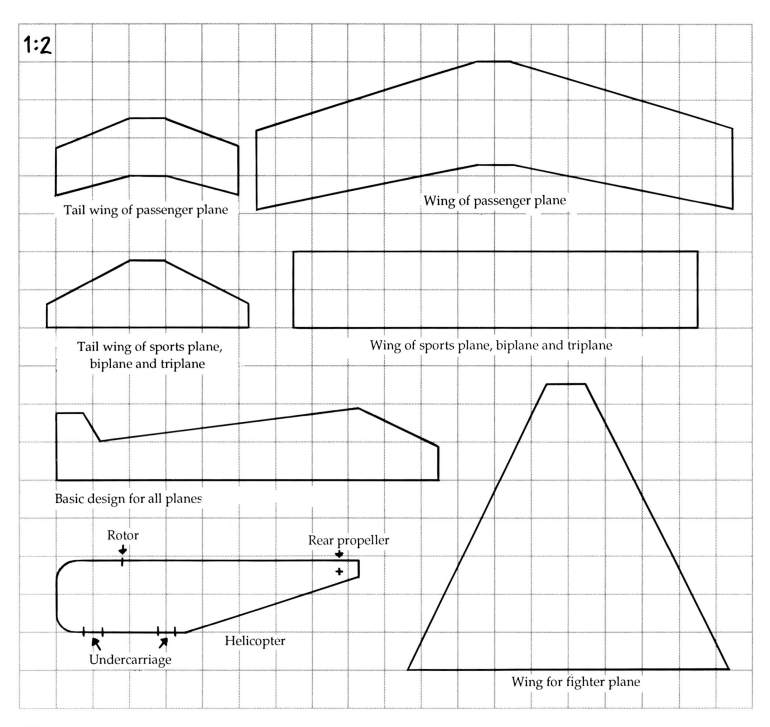

Tail wing of passenger plane

Wing of passenger plane

Tail wing of sports plane,
biplane and triplane

Wing of sports plane, biplane and triplane

Basic design for all planes

Rotor

Rear propeller

Helicopter

Undercarriage

Wing for fighter plane

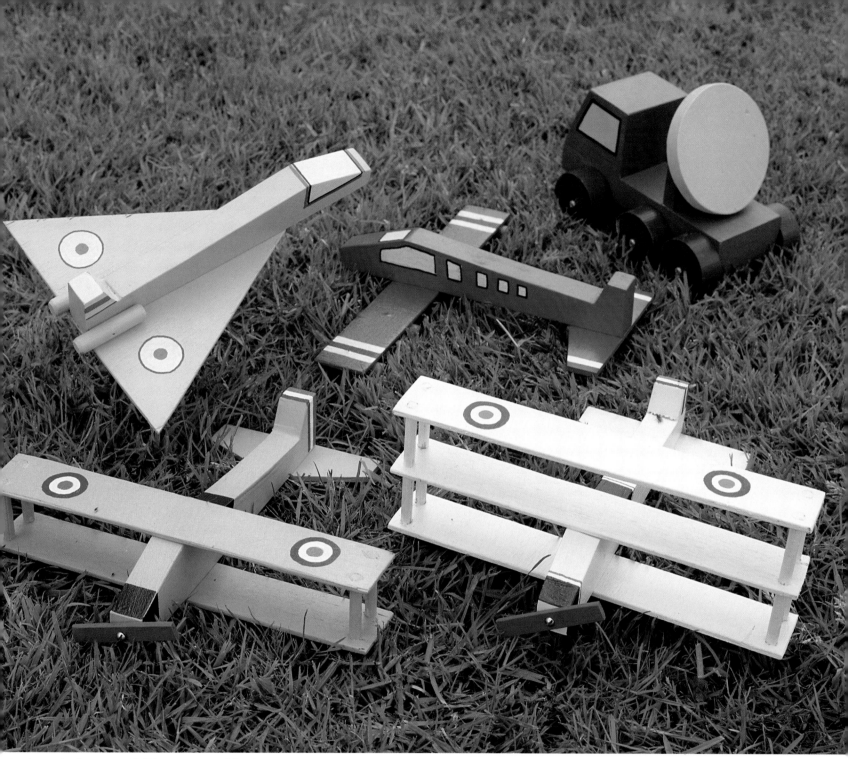

Radar vehicle, page 27. Planes, pages 39–42.

Vintage planes [41]

Both biplanes and triplanes have connected wings which are cut from from 4 mm plywood, 4x22 cm. The distance between the wings should be 3.5 cm. Drill holes in the four corners of the wings as shown in the illustration. For the struts between the wings you can use welding wire or thin dowel, about 3 mm in diameter. Make the propeller from an ice lolly stick, 6 cm long and 5 mm wide.

Sports plane

The sports plane has wings made from 4 mm plywood, 4x22 cm. The aircraft should also have a propeller; see description under vintage planes.

Helicopter

Cut out the body of the helicopter in accordance with the template on page 40. Make the undercarriage from two strips of wood, 1x1x5 cm, and nail them under the body of the helicopter (see illustration). The two sticks fastened laterally underneath are 1x1x8 cm. The long rotor blade, which should be 10 mm wide and 14 cm long, is made from an ice lolly stick or 4 mm plywood, as is the propeller, which should be 10 mm wide and 4 cm long. Attach the propeller and rotor blade with nails.

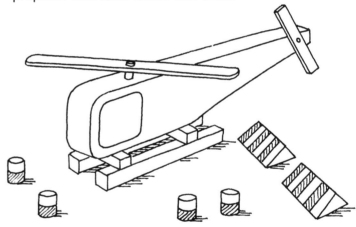

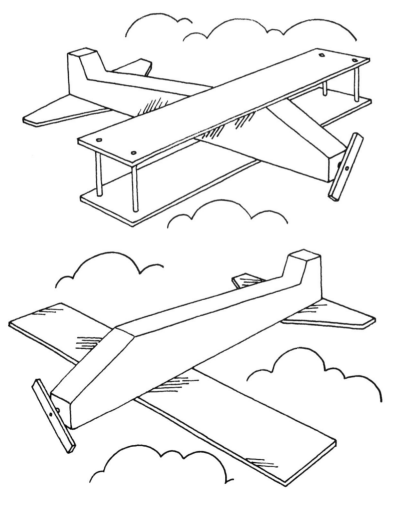

Decoration

You can paint the aircraft in a variety of colours. Civilian aircraft can be silver coloured with black windows. Military planes can be painted in camouflage colours — brown, green and black. Paint jet engines black at the front and red towards the rear, so that they look as though they are in operation. You can also paint the aircraft in bright colours as shown in the illustration on page 41.

FARM ANIMALS [45]

If you are making the farm on page 22 you will also need some animals. In this section you will find templates for making the most common farm animals out of pine. Cut out the animals with a coping saw. This may well take a great deal of patience if the wood is too thick, but at the same time, be careful not to use wood that is too thin because the models will not stay upright.

MATERIALS AND TOOLS:
Pine, 18 mm
String (for the tail)
Drill
Coping saw
Wood file

The templates are drawn to a scale of 1:1. Transfer the animals to the wood and cut them out. If you want to avoid having to deal with the uneven sections such as the crest of the hen and cock and the body of the sheep, simply round off the models and draw in the curved lines as contours when you come to decorate the animals later.

If you have the time and the inclination, you can round off the animals at the front and back with a wood file or piece of sandpaper so that they look less angular. If you are cutting the animals from thicker wood — 32 mm, for example — it is possible to cut out the legs and ears, as shown in the illustration, but make sure that the wood does not split. If you feel that the small animals are too wide, you could possibly saw them down the middle so that you finish with two animals instead of one.

Decoration

As you can see from the templates on the next page, it is possible to give some of the animals tails made of string. The animals should also be painted. The horse's body can, for example, be painted brown, grey or black. The saddle and harness can be painted in a contrasting colour. Use string to make the tail and mane. The cow's body can be painted black and white, or red-brown. The tail is made of string. The teats are four small tacks with round heads tapped up into the udder. Paint the pig's body pink. The tail is a short piece of string tied in a curl. Decorate the other animals in suitable colours.

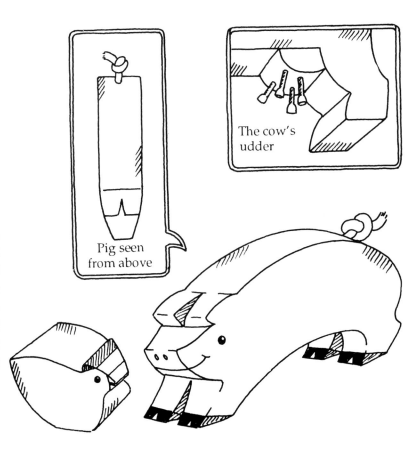

The cow's udder

Pig seen from above

1:1

Farm, page 22. Church, page 23. Farm animals, pages 43–44.
Tanker, page 28. Tractor, page 30.

PUPPETS [49]

Figures that move with the aid of string are called puppets. All the puppets in this section are animals, which you can make 'perform'.

MATERIALS AND TOOLS:
Plywood, 9 mm
Fishing line
Strips of pine
Thick string
Coping saw
Drill

The templates are drawn to a scale of 1:2. The figures, which consist of a head, body and two feet, are drawn onto the wood and cut out. Decorate the different parts. Use thick string for the neck and legs. The length will depend on the model. Drill holes for the neck in the lower part of the head and the upper part of the body. The diameter of the holes should match the thickness of the string, which should be glued in. To make the legs thread the pieces of string into the respective holes in the body and feet and glue them in place.

You should also drill holes in the top of the body and head as shown on the template. These two holes are for attaching the string used to control the figure. Tie two pieces of string to the legs as well, as shown in the illustration. The four strings go up to a cross made from strips of wood. The cross should be approximately 20 cm long and 10 cm wide. Attach the strings to the crosspieces as shown in the illustration.

Decoration

Paint the different parts so that both sides are identical; see the templates.

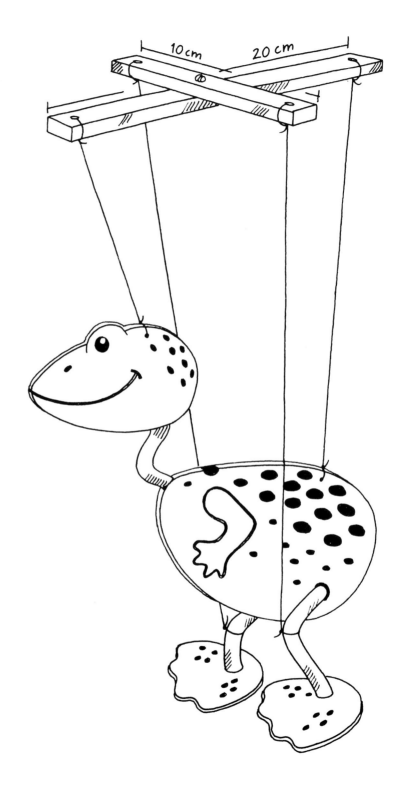

1:2

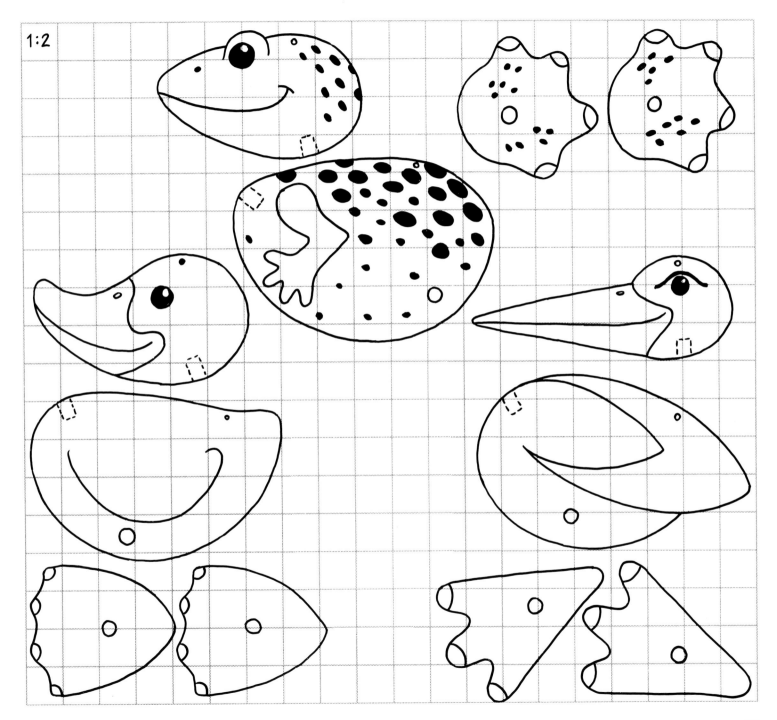

47

CLIMBING FIGURES [49]

These figures can climb up and down two pieces of string when you pull the bottom. The pieces of string run through holes in the arms of the figure.

MATERIALS AND TOOLS:
Plywood, 9 mm
Nylon cord, 2–3 mm
Dowel, 9 mm
Wooden beads, 20–30 mm in diameter
Drill
Coping saw

The templates are drawn to a scale of 1:2. Transfer the figure to the wood and cut it out. The dotted lines on the template show where the holes should be drilled. These holes should be 3–4 mm in diameter and should be drilled right through. The piece of dowel for hanging should be 11–12 cm long and have two holes drilled in it as shown in the illustration. The distance between the holes in the figure and in the piece of dowel should be identical. The holes should have a diameter of 3 mm and be drilled right through. Pull the two pieces of cord, each about 50 cm long, through their respective holes in the dowel. Tie a knot underneath to stop them running through the holes. Tie the ends at the top as shown in the illustration. Run the other two ends through the holes in the figure's arms and attach a bead at the bottom of each cord. Hang the stick so that it can swing from side to side. If you pull the cords one at a time, the figure will climb up. When it has reached the top, let go the cords and it will slide down to the bottom. Then start all over again.

Decoration

You can let your imagination have full rein when you decorate these figures. You can also paint the reverse side and show what they look like from behind.

Puppets, pages 46–47.

Climbing figures, pages 48–50.

1:2

ANIMALS ON WHEELS [53]

Animals on wheels are ideal for small children who like to push them along. Make them from pine and decorate them in amusing colours.

MATERIALS AND TOOLS:
Plywood, 12 mm
Pine, 25 mm
Dowel, 10 mm
String
Drill
Coping saw

The templates are drawn to a scale of 1:3. Draw the figure onto the wood and cut it out. The wheels can be cut from dowels or plywood. For most of the animals the wheels should be 45 mm in diameter and about 15 mm thick. However, the two wheels on the crocodile are 30 mm in diameter, as are the rear wheels of the dragon. The front wheels of the dragon are 60 mm. To attach the wheels use a piece of 10 mm dowel as an axle. The hole for the axle in the figure itself should be about 11 mm in diameter. Cut the horse, zebra and giraffe from a single piece of wood. Use string for the tails. Because the giraffe is so tall, it is a good idea to put three or four washers between the wheels and the legs to give the figure a broader base to stand on and help prevent it from falling over.

The tail of the whale is made of leather and is fitted into a horizontal groove sawn into the body. Cut the ears of the elephant out of thin plywood and attach them with hinges. You can also make the ears from leather. The wings of the dragon move up and down as the wheels turn. This is because the big wheels are arranged with an offset centre. The axle for the wings is a thin piece of dowel. Saw the arms from thin plywood and nail them in place. The upper jaw of the crocodile is sawn from thicker wood than the body itself — 32 mm pine, for example. Fit the jaw with a small hinge (see illustration). The front wheels are attached with an offset centre. The axle should be positioned so that the jaw rests on the two front wheels. As the wheels turn, the mouth opens and closes.

Decoration

Decorate the animals as shown on the templates. You do not need to use the traditional colours. For example, you could paint the elephant pink and the whale blue if you wished.

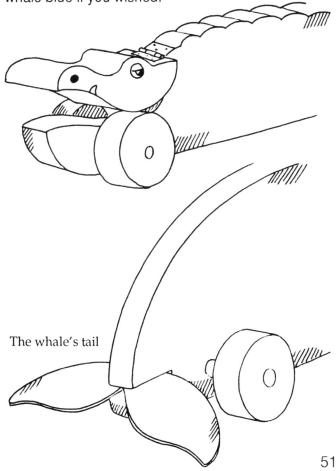

The whale's tail

Animals on wheels, pages 51–52.

FLYING BIRDS — AND OTHER ANIMALS

The models in this section look very lifelike as they glide up and down. They can hang from the ceiling and when you give them a light pull, they move their wings gracefully. The bodies follow the rhythm of the wings and move gently too.

MATERIALS AND TOOLS:
Plywood, 6 mm
Nylon cord, 2–3 mm
Dowel, 10 mm
Wooden bead, 2–3 cm
Drill
Coping saw

The designs are drawn to a scale of 1:3, but you can make the models larger or smaller without affecting the function. Each model requires a body and two wings.

After cutting out the body and wings in 6 mm plywood, drill the holes for assembly and hanging. The position of these holes can vary slightly, and it is best to assemble the figure and try hanging it in a couple of loops first as shown in the illustration. You will need someone to help you check the position of the cords and mark where the wings hang correctly.

The piece of dowel for hanging should be roughly half as long as the distance between the wing tips. Attach the cord to the wings and lead it up to the dowel as shown. Drill holes in the dowel to thread the cord through. Don't cut off the cords until you are sure the model is balanced when hanging.

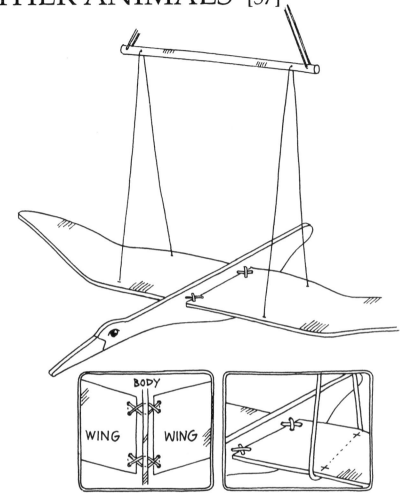

Decoration

Use your imagination when you decorate the different animals. Paint the dragon light green, and use brilliant colours for the parrot. Instead of a wooden bead to pull the string, try using a wooden egg if the model is a bird.

1:3

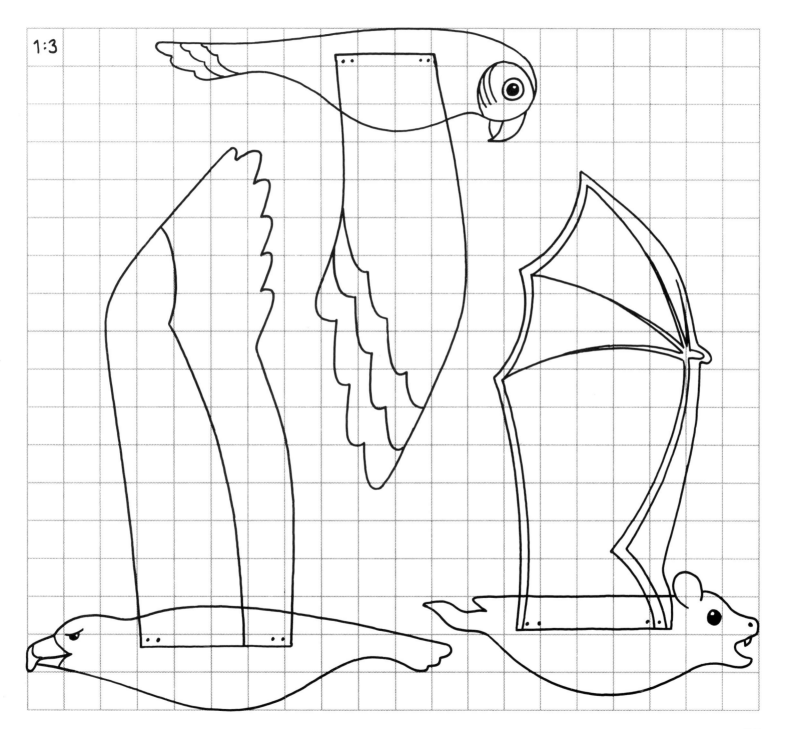

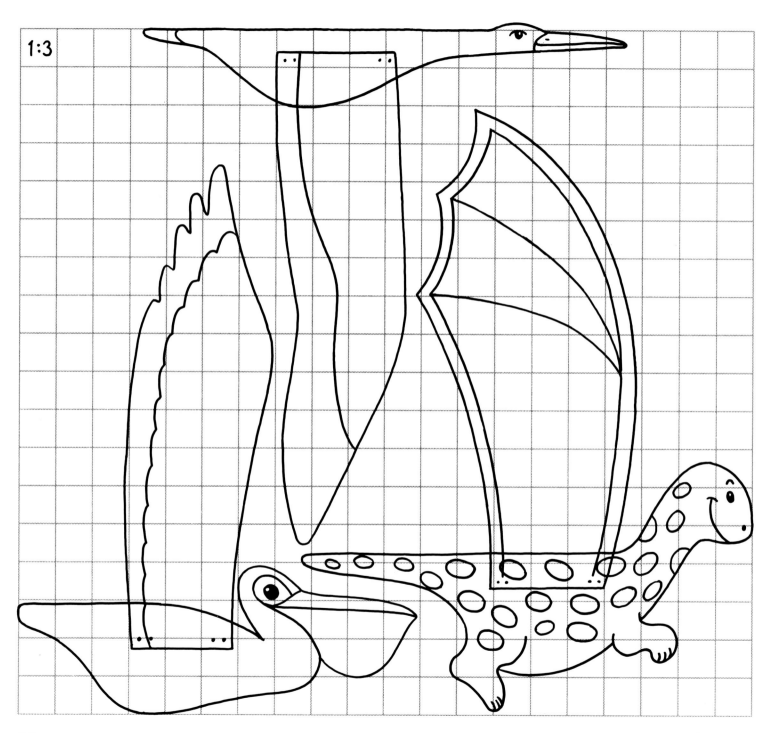

1:3

Dragon, pages 54–56.

Bat, pages 54–56.

Stork, pages 54–56.

Parrot, pages 54–56.

HOBBYHORSES [61]

The hobbyhorse is a traditional wooden toy that is still popular today. But you don't just have to make horses — there are many other possibilities. The templates on the following pages will give you ideas for both wild and farm animals. For example, you could make a billy-goat or a giraffe with a spotted neck.

MATERIALS AND TOOLS:
Loose thread
Dowel, 22 mm
Plywood, 9 mm
Drill
Fretsaw

The templates are drawn to a scale of 1:4. Transfer the head to a piece of plywood, 24x24 cm, and cut it out. The hole marked on the template shows where the rein is to be placed. Drill through this hole, then mount the head on a piece of dowel about 90 cm long. The best way to attach the head is to cut a groove, 9 mm wide and 4 cm deep, in the stick. Press the head down into the groove along the dotted lines on the template (see illustration). Glue the head in position.

It can be difficult for children to cut a groove in the stick without splitting it, so here is an easier method. Attach the stick to one side of the head with two electrician's fittings. Attach the fittings with small screws (see bottom illustration). If you are going to try this method, it is best to use thicker plywood — 12 mm, for example. One disadvantage is that the animal has a 'back', but you can camouflage that when you come to decorate it.

Decoration

If the animal has a characteristic pattern, you could perhaps decorate the stick in the same way as the head. For example, you could paint spots on the neck of the giraffe or stripes on the neck of the zebra. As you can see from the illustration below, you can drill holes to make a mane for the zebra and horse. The mane consists of pieces of thread, attached as shown. You can also make some of the animals' eyes out of pieces of leather. When you have finished decorating the hobbyhorse, push the rein through the hole.

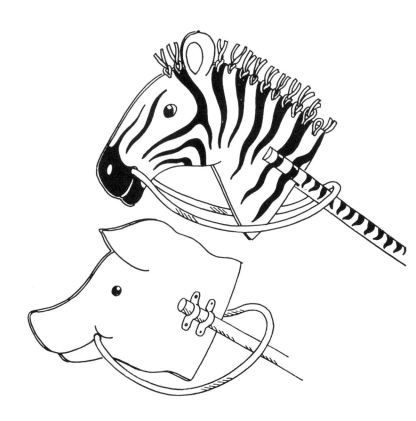

1:4

59

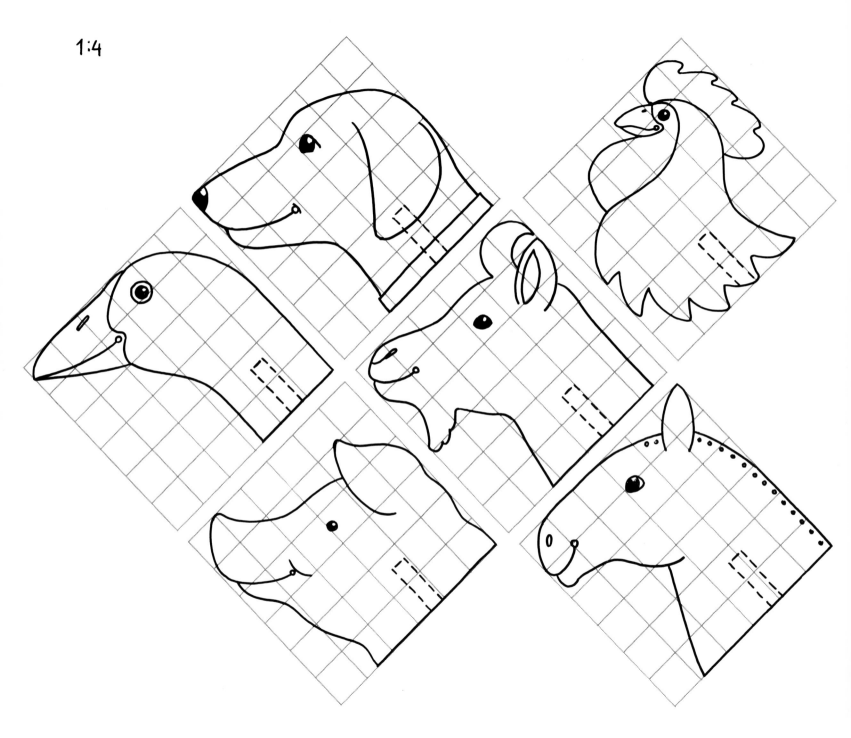

rses, page 58–60.

FLAPPERS [65]

These animals are so called because they have leather or vinyl feet rather like small flappers attached to wheels. As the animal goes along it says 'Flap, flap'. In some toy shops you can buy a 'flapping duck', but you won't often find moles, hares, frogs, penguins and puffins as you do in this section.

MATERIALS AND TOOLS:
Pine, 19 mm
Dowel, 10 mm
Vinyl or leather
Drill
Coping saw
Handsaw

The designs are drawn to a scale of 1:2. Transfer the model to the wood. The hole for the wheel axle, 11 mm in diameter, is marked on the template. Cut the wheels from round wood or pine. They should be about 45 mm in diameter and roughly 20 mm thick.

Cut the feet from vinyl or leather. Fit them to the wheels in separate sections as shown in the illustration. The feet should be at 180 degrees to each other in order to create the 'flapping' effect. You can also position the feet of the hare and frog so that it looks as though they are hopping.

To make the wheel axles as strong as possible it is best to drill right through both wheels. The axle should be about 45 mm long. This gives roughly 12–13 mm between the wheels and the body (see the illustration). Glue the axle to one wheel and push it through the hole in the body. Then glue on the other wheel.

Make the steering bar from a 10 mm piece of dowel, approximately 50 cm long. Drill a hole in the model about 40 mm deep as indicated by the dotted line on the template. Glue the steering bar into the hole. If you wish you can fit a handle to the end of the bar.

Decoration

When you paint the bodies use colours that are suitable for the animal concerned. Paint the hare's body brown, grey or white. Paint the mole's body grey-black, and its nose and paws bright red. Paint the front of the puffin's body white and the back black. The large head section should be white, and the bill red, yellow and blue. Paint the front of the penguin's body white and the back black. The bill should be yellow. The duck's body should be white and the bill yellow. Paint the whole of the frog's body light green with dark green spots.

1:2

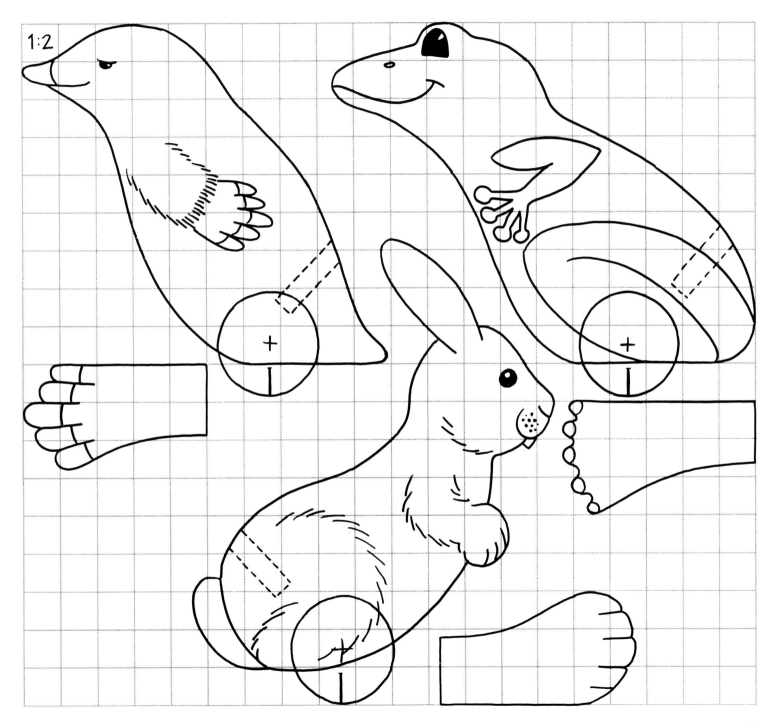

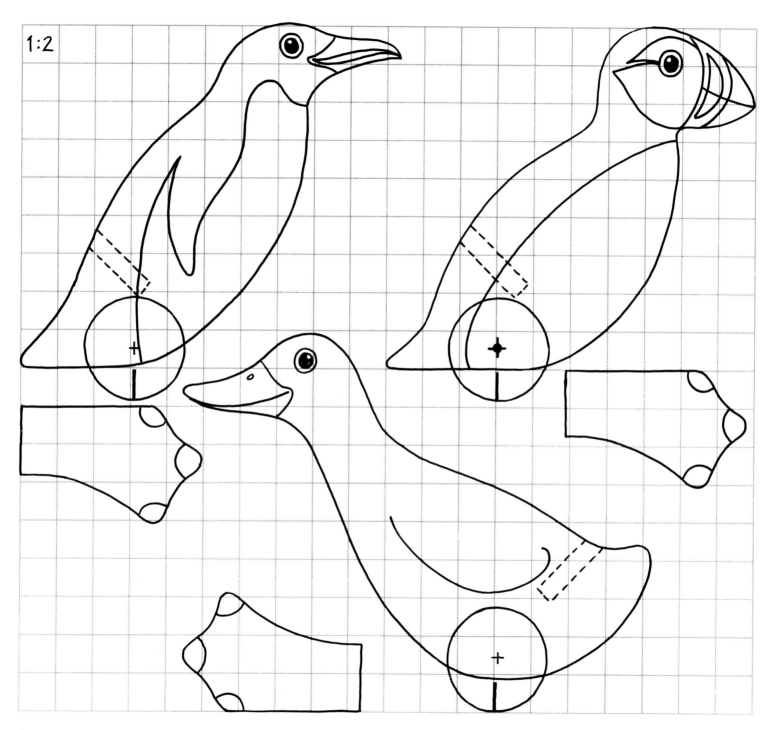

1:2

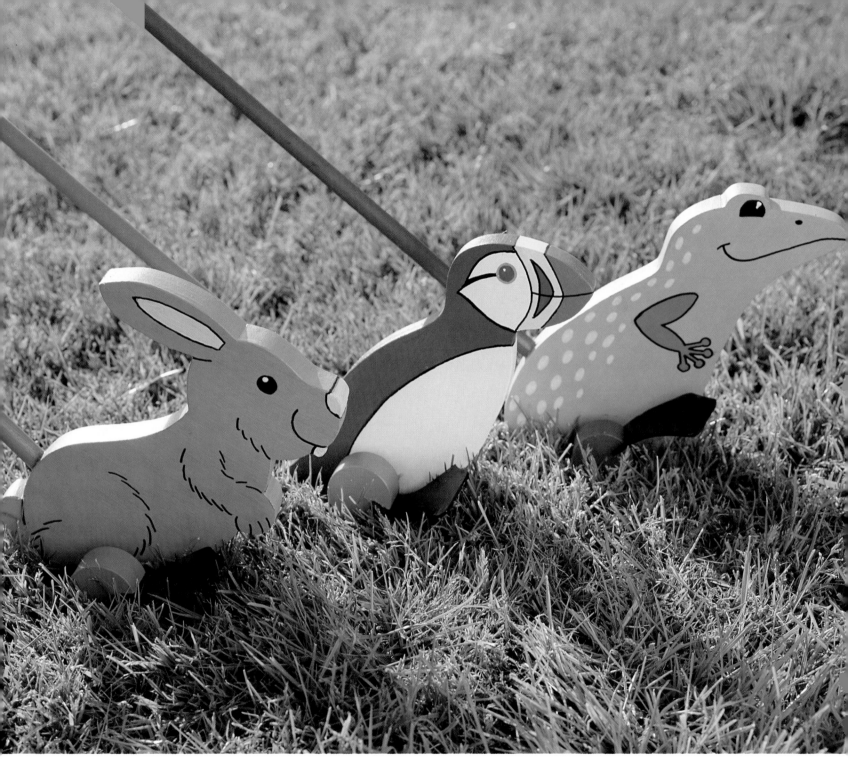

Flappers, pages 62–64

ACROBATS [69]

The acrobat hangs on a small stand, made from a length of dowel. When you press the bottom of the stand, the acrobat swings round and performs some amusing tricks. Instead of an acrobat you can also make other figures as shown on the templates.

MATERIALS AND TOOLS:
Dowel, 6 and 10 mm
Cotton thread
Plywood, 4 mm
Drill
Fretsaw
Hand saw

The templates are drawn to a scale of 1:1. The figures are quite small so it is important to use a good quality plywood such as birch, otherwise the wood may splinter. Each figure will need a body, two arms and two legs. Drill holes in the arms, legs and body as indicated on the templates. The holes should be 2 mm in diameter. Tie the arms and legs to the body with strong cotton. Tie a knot on either side so that the various parts can move freely.

The frame is made from two pieces of dowel, 10 mm in diameter and 22.5 cm long. You will also need a cross-bar, which is made from 6 mm dowel, 6 cm long. Assemble the stand as shown in the illustration, drilling the cross-bar into the two vertical sticks. Drill two holes, 2 mm in diameter, at the top of the sticks. Attach the figure to the stand by running a piece of thread through the holes in the top of the arms. The thread must be loose enough to cross over but not so loose as to allow the figure to hang. If you like, you can place a small wooden bead on the thread between the arms to hold them apart. If you

press the bottom of the stand, you will make the figure swing round.

Decoration

You do not need to paint the stand itself but the figures should be decorated so that they look amusing and interesting. The acrobat should have a striped top and trousers and a black moustache. The girl artiste should have a bright skirt with pink border and golden hair and a red mouth. Give the clown a white outfit and a red mouth and nose. The monkey has a dark brown body and light brown head. The bear should have a golden brown body.

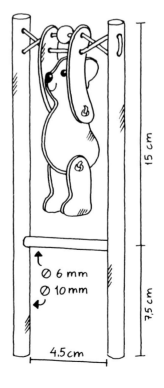

15 cm

7,5 cm

Ø 6 mm
Ø 10 mm

4.5 cm

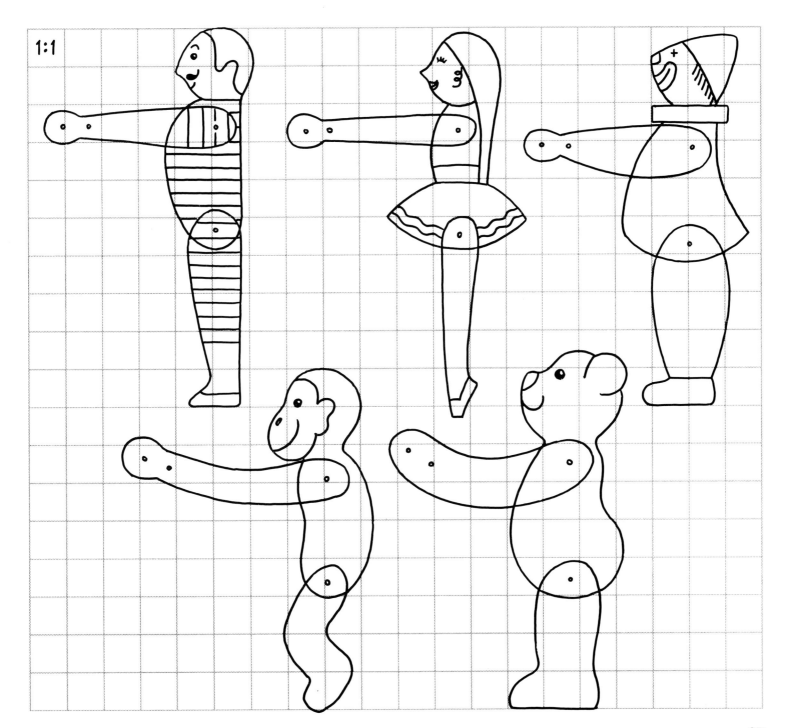

1:1

BALANCING FIGURES [69]

The point about the figures in this section is that they always keep their balance. You can turn them round as much as you like but they will always find their way back to their original position.

MATERIALS AND TOOLS:
Cotton thread or nylon cord
Plywood, 19 mm
Dowel, 10 mm
Drill
Coping saw

The templates are drawn to a scale of 1:3. Transfer the figure to the wood and cut it out. Drill holes through the feet of the birds or the hands of the clown or acrobat, as shown on the templates on page 70. The hole should be about 11 mm in diameter. For hanging use two pieces of dowel, about 20 cm long. Drill holes, 3–4 mm in diameter, through both pieces of dowel about 2 cm from the ends. Push one stick through the hole in the figure, making sure that it can rotate unhindered. To hang the figure run the thread through the two sticks as shown in the illustration. If you test the figure when it is hanging by turning it upside down, you should find that it will revert to its starting position. If you have a big metal ring that can be opened, you could also use that to hang the figure on.

Decoration
The birds should be brightly-coloured like real parrots. Use your imagination when you are painting the clown, but the acrobat should perhaps be slightly more subdued.

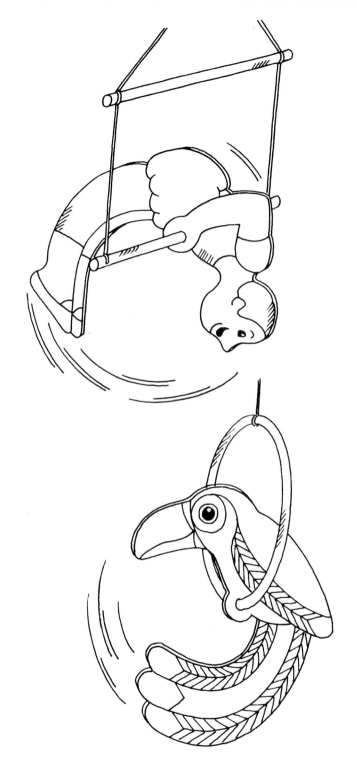

Parrots, pages 68–70.

Clown, pages 68–70.

Acrobats, pages 66–67.

1:3

TUMBLERS [73]

Tumblers have always been popular toys. The best known type of tumbler is the puppet with the thick, round body, which always stands up again no matter how often you try to push it down. It is impossible to tip it over. The tumblers described in this section can also rock from side to side. However, if they fall either backwards or forwards, they will not stand up again on their own. Even so, they make splendid toys or decorations.

MATERIALS AND TOOLS:
Pine, 2–3 cm
Plywood, 4 mm
Coping saw

The templates are drawn to a scale of 1:3. You can transfer the figure to a piece of pine, 30x15 cm. The wood can be 25 mm thick, for example. The little attachments for the figures are drawn on 4 mm plywood. You should make four for each figure. Drill small holes in them as shown in the illustration. When you have decorated the models, screw the attachments to the arms as shown. It is important to make sure that the diameter of the holes is slightly larger than the screws, so that they can hang freely. At the same time do not put the screws in so tightly that the attachments cannot move. They should remain vertical as the figure rocks from side to side.

Decoration

Transfer the outlines from the templates to the wood. Decorate the individual figures as follows. Harlequin has a black cap and mask, a white shirt frill, a check costume in bright colours and a gold belt, if desired. Columbine has golden hair, red cheeks and lips, a bright dress with red or pink roses and a pink top. Pierrot has a white hat and costume, a red mouth and black eyebrows, black buttons and shoes. The goblin girl has golden hair, red cheeks and lips, a red dress and a white apron with yellow stars. The goblin boy has red cheeks, a red cap with a white bobble, a red waistcoat with a white trim, a grey shirt under the waistcoat and a black belt with a yellow heart.

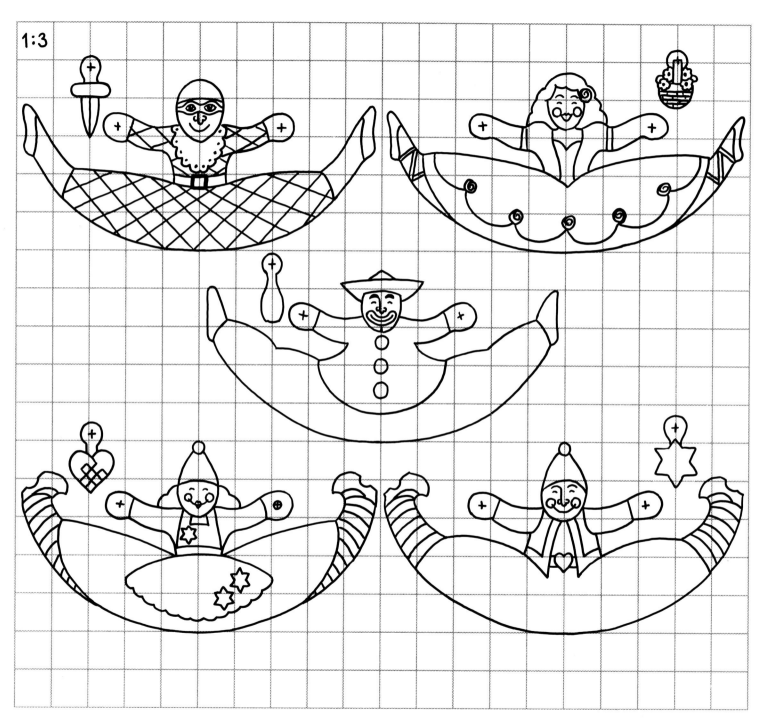

1:3

Tumblers, page 71–72.

FOUR IN A ROW [77]

Four In A Row is a game whose object is to place four rings in a straight row — horizontally, vertically or diagonally (see the illustration below). There are two players, each with 21 rings of a chosen colour — red and white, for example. The rings are to be placed over seven sticks, which are fixed to a base (see below). The participants take turns to place a ring. As explained above, the object of the game is to end up with four rings in a straight row, while at the same time managing to prevent your opponent from the doing the same.

MATERIALS AND TOOLS:
Pine, 19 mm
Dowel, 10 and 28 mm
Drill
Hand saw

The base section should be 12x28 cm. Drill 7 holes in the board, 10 mm in diameter, as shown in the illustration. You must be very careful when drilling to make sure that the holes are absolutely symmetrical, otherwise you may find that the dowel is not absolutely vertical. The sticks should be 15 cm long. Glue them into the holes. To make the rings, saw 42 discs from a piece of round wood, 28 mm in diameter. The best way to do this is in a mitre box. The discs should be about 1 cm thick. In the middle of each disc drill a hole at least 11 mm in diameter. Instead of using a piece of round wood, you can also cut out the discs from square blocks.

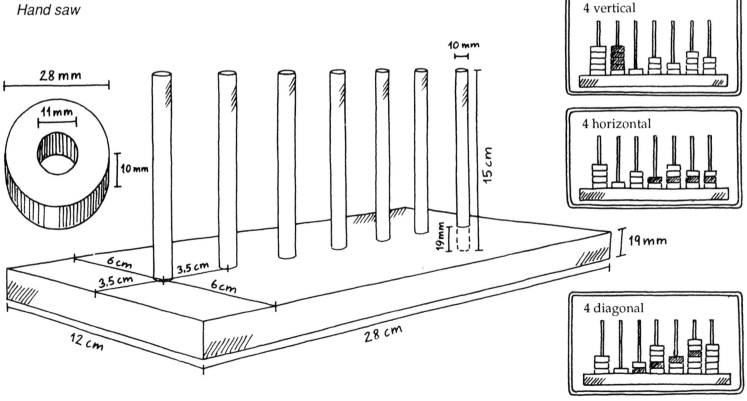

74

MOVE THE PYRAMID [77]

Move The Pyramid is somewhat similar to Four In A Row, but in this game there is only one player — you are your own opponent. For this game you need a base with three sticks. On one of the outer sticks you place a number of pieces — say, three — to form a pyramid. The object of the game is to move those three pieces to the other outer stick via the middle stick, but without at any time placing a large piece above a smaller one. If you are clever, you can transfer all three pieces in seven moves. To make the game more challenging, you could, for example, use seven pieces. But bear in mind that if you do that the smallest number of moves you can take to win is 127, so it's probably better in the beginning to start with fewer pieces.

MATERIALS AND TOOLS:
Plywood, 9 mm
Pine, 19 mm
Dowel, 10 mm
Drill
Hand saw

Make the base section from pine, 12x28 cm. Drill holes, 10 mm in diameter, in the board as shown. Glue the three pieces of dowel, 15 cm long, into the holes.

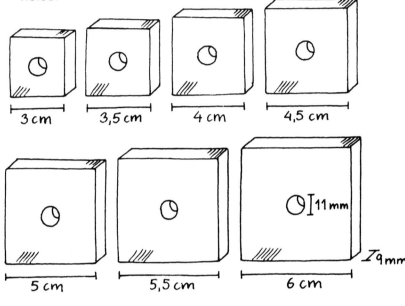

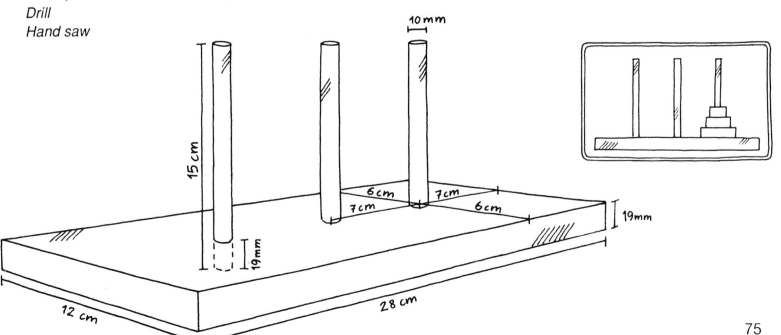

BALL GAME WITH GATEWAYS [77]

This ball game is great fun and easy to make. In the old days it used to be a very popular game and was played with clay balls or marbles. Owners of ball games challenged each other. The players took their positions about 2 meters from the game, which was placed on the ground. The object of the game was to roll the balls through the gateways. If you managed to do this, you received the number of points that was indicated by the figure over that particular hole. All balls that ran past went to the owner of the game.

MATERIALS AND TOOLS:
Plywood, 9 mm
Pine, 19 mm
Centre bit
Coping saw
Hand saw

Cut the front section from plywood, 10x40 cm. The two end pieces are a piece of plywood, 10x10 cm, sawn diagonally to create two triangles. Cut out the gateways as shown in the illustration. If you prefer, you can make the arches by using a centre bit and then sawing from the edge up to the hole (see illustration). Alternatively, you can cut out the entire gateway with a coping saw. If you do not want the game to be too easy, make sure that openings are not too big. Glue and nail the edge sections at each end.

Decoration
After you have painted the game, write in the points figure over the gateways as shown in the illustration. The gateway in the middle offers the highest number of points.

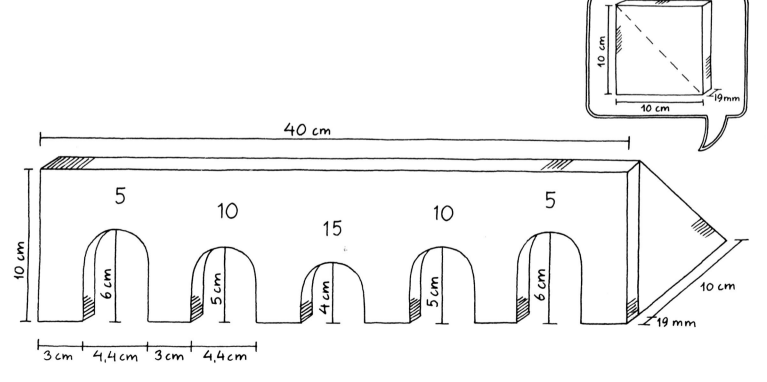

Four In A Row, page 74. Move The Pyramid, page 75.
Ball Game With Gateways, page 76. Sloping Ball Game, page 78.

SLOPING BALL GAME [77]

This game is similar to the last one in that it involves rolling balls. The game consists of a sloping base with holes. This is placed on the ground. The object of the game is to roll the balls and try to make them drop in the holes. Each hole has a number over it to indicate the score in points. Whoever gains the most points wins the game.

MATERIALS AND TOOLS
Plywood, 18 mm
Strip of wood, 2x2 cm
Centre bit
Hand saw

Saw the base plate from plywood, 25x30 cm. Drill five holes in the plate using a centre bit (see illustration). The holes should be about 5 cm in diameter. Plane or smooth the lower edge of the board so that it runs down at an angle. It is very important to make the surface completely smooth so that the balls will roll over it. To make sure that the base stands at an angle, glue and nail a strip of wood, 2x2 cm, under the top edge of the plate, as shown in the illustration. If you want to make it easier to check which hole a particular ball has gone through, you can sew some bags and glue them underneath the holes. Or you could use small rubber balls that cannot roll out of the holes because they are too big.

Decoration
Paint the game and write the score indicators above the holes.

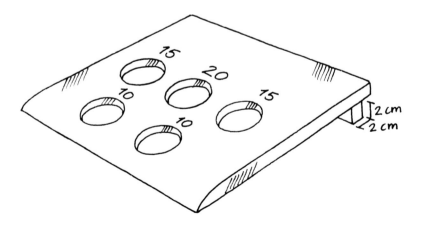

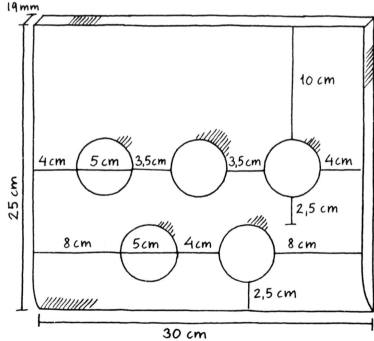